MW01611933

sim ply delicious slices

Your Promise of Success

Welcome to the world of Confident Cooking, created for you in
our **Test Kitchen,** where recipes are double-tested by our team
of home economists to achieve a high standard of success.

MURDOCH BOOKS®

Sydney • London • Vancouver • New York

SLICE BASICS

With a few basic techniques, these all-occasion treats are great for the beginner and experienced cook alike. The result can be popped into a lunchbox or served with lashings of cream as the grand finale to a special meal.

EQUIP YOURSELF

To accurately measure your tin, turn it up-side down and measure the base. We use a variety of tin sizes in our recipes and, obviously, not every kitchen will have all of them, but don't let that put you off. If you don't have the exact size, use the closest you have and adjust the cooking time. If you have the choice, go for a slightly larger tin—the mixture will spread out a little more thinly and take less time to cook. In a smaller tin, the mixture is likely to bubble up over the top, so place a tray under it to catch the drips. It may also take a little longer to cook. A tin that is too small will make a thicker, more cake-like base, not a chewy one. But, be careful, if the tin is much too large, the base may be dry and brittle.

Tins with a dark interior are usually non-stick, meaning your slice will cook in less time and brown more quickly—check the slice for doneness about 5 minutes before the end of the cooking time given in the recipe.

LINING THE TIN

It is always a good idea to line the tin with baking paper. This has a dual purpose: to prevent the slice from sticking to the tin, and to provide 'handles' so you can lift it easily out of the tin.

Grease the base and sides with butter or oil spray, then line the base with a piece of non-stick baking paper. The paper should neatly fit the base of the tin, without creases, and should be wide enough to allow an 'overhanging handle' along two opposite sides.

Some recipes may only require the base to be lined—place the tin on a piece of baking paper, trace around the outside edge and cut out.

If all four sides of the tin need to be lined, simply line the base, overhanging two sides, then lay another piece of paper over the top, overhanging the other two sides.

PERFECT PASTRY

In most recipes the ingredients are best used at room temperature, but when making pastry, the butter should be diced then well chilled. Also, when rubbing the butter into the flour, try to use just your fingertips as they are cooler than the rest of your hands.

IN THE OVEN

Some recipes ask for a pastry base to be partially baked before the topping or filling is added. This is called 'blind baking' and ensures the base stays firm or crisp and not made soggy by the filling. Once the uncooked pastry is in the tin, cover with a sheet of baking paper, fill with baking beads or uncooked rice, then bake. Remove the beads and cook the pastry again until lightly golden and dry. The base is now ready for the topping and final baking. If the top of the slice starts to overbrown during cooking, cover loosely with foil or baking paper.

For best results, bake in the centre (away from the sides) on the middle rack of the oven, to allow the heat to circulate properly and the slice to cook evenly.

Hints and Tips

● Toasting nuts before use enhances their flavour. Spread on a baking tray and toast in a moderate 180°C (350°F/Gas 4) oven for 5-8 minutes, or until lightly coloured.

● Nuts contain essential oils which have a tendency to go rancid at room temperature. For long-term storage, keep in a tightly sealed bag or airtight container in the freezer.

● When shredding or grating rind, use only the coloured surface of the peel, not the spongy white pith—this is bitter.

● To finely grate the rind, place a piece of baking paper over the grater— this prevents rind getting caught in the holes.

● Use your fingers or the back of a spoon to evenly press the mixture in the tin.

● Pierce the slice with a skewer to check that it's cooked—it should come out clean. Some slices firm up in the tin once left to cool.

● Cut chocolate-topped slices with a hot knife. Dip the knife into boiling water, then wipe dry before cutting.

● To cut evenly into squares, diamonds or fingers, use a ruler as a guide. Wipe the knife clean after each cut.

● Cool slices completely before storing in an airtight container.

INDULGENT SLICES

There's nothing quite like a piece or two of homemade slice with a cup of coffee for afternoon tea—or for a snack ...

ALMOND CHEWS

Prep time: 15 minutes
Cooking time: 45 minutes
Makes 35 pieces

160 g unsalted butter
11/4 cups (310 g) caster sugar
1/4 cup (45 g) soft brown sugar
2 eggs
3 teaspoons vanilla essence
2 cups (250 g) self-raising flour
150 g white chocolate, chopped
150 g flaked almonds
icing sugar, for dusting

1 Lightly grease a 30 x 20 cm shallow baking tin and line the base and sides with baking paper, leaving the paper hanging over the two long sides—this makes it easier to lift the cooked slice out of the tin.
2 Place the butter, caster sugar and soft brown sugar in a saucepan and stir over low heat until the butter melts and the sugars dissolve. Remove from the heat and leave to cool. Preheat the oven to warm 170°C (325°F/Gas 3).
3 Place the eggs in a bowl and beat with electric beaters until thick and pale. Add the vanilla essence, flour and cooled butter mixture and mix well. Stir in the chocolate and half the almonds. Spread into the tin and sprinkle the remaining almonds over the surface. Bake for 40 minutes, or until golden. The centre will be soft and chewy. Leave to cool in the tin, then lift out and trim the edges. Dust with the icing sugar and cut into 4 cm squares.

Nutrition per piece: Fat 8 g; Protein 3 g; Carbohydrate 18 g; Dietary Fibre 0.5 g; Cholesterol 22.5 mg; 620 kJ (150 cal)

Almond chews

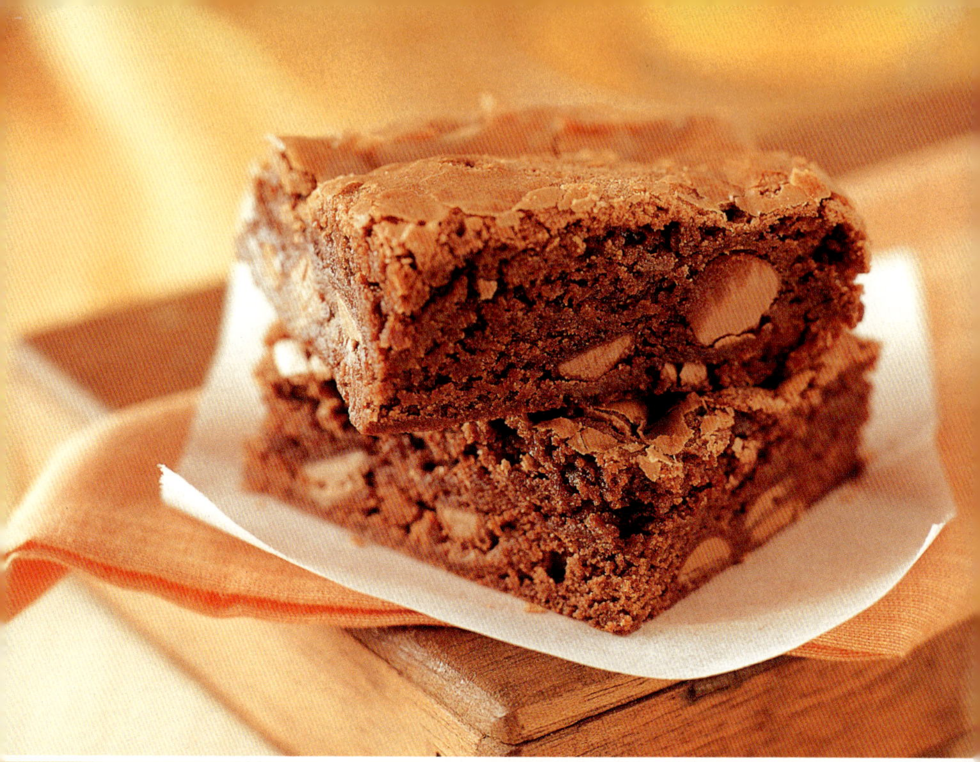

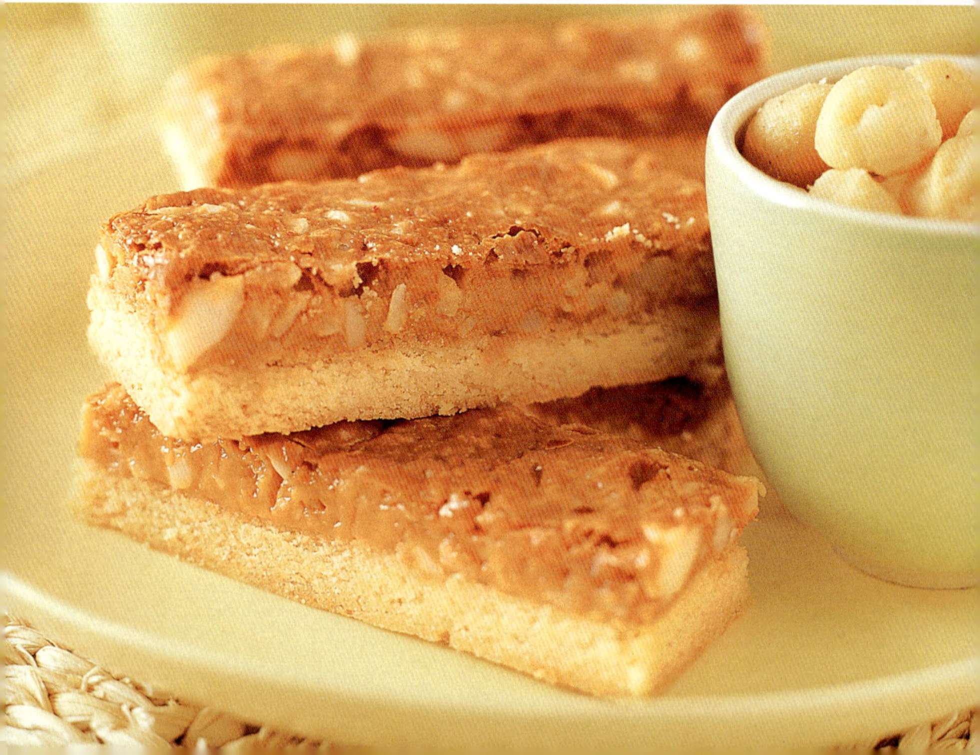

CLASSIC BROWNIES

Prep time: 15 minutes
Cooking time: 20 minutes
Makes 16 pieces

1 cup (125 g) plain flour
1/2 teaspoon baking powder
150 g dark chocolate
90 g unsalted butter
2 eggs, lightly beaten
3/4 cup (185 g) caster sugar
1 teaspoon vanilla essence
100 g milk choc chips

1 Preheat the oven to moderate 180°C (350°F/Gas 4). Lightly grease a shallow 20 cm square cake tin and line the base and sides with baking paper, leaving the paper hanging over two opposite sides.

2 Sift the flour and baking powder together. Chop the chocolate and butter into small even-sized pieces and put in a heatproof bowl. Bring a medium saucepan of water to the boil, then remove from the heat. Sit the bowl over the pan, making sure the bowl doesn't touch the water. Allow to stand, stirring occasionally, until the chocolate and butter have melted. Leave to cool slightly.

3 Place the eggs, sugar and vanilla essence in a bowl and beat with electric beaters for 2 minutes, or until pale and thick. Add the melted chocolate and butter and stir to combine. Fold in the flour with a metal spoon until combined, then add the choc chips and mix well. Pour into the tin and bake for 20 minutes, or until a skewer inserted in the centre comes out clean. Leave to cool in the tin for 10 minutes then lift out onto a wire rack and cool completely. Cut into squares using a sharp knife.

Nutrition per piece: Fat 10 g; Protein 3 g; Carbohydrate 27 g; Dietary Fibre 0.5 g; Cholesterol 38 mg; 850 kJ (205 cal)

MACADAMIA FINGERS

Prep time: 15 minutes
Cooking time: 1 hour
Makes 18 pieces

180 g unsalted butter, softened
1 teaspoon vanilla essence
1/3 cup (90 g) caster sugar
2 cups (250 g) plain flour, sifted
120 g unsalted butter, extra
2 x 395 g cans condensed milk
2 tablespoons golden syrup
1 1/4 cups (200 g) macadamia nuts, coarsely chopped

1 Preheat the oven to moderate 180°C (350°F/Gas 4). Lightly grease a shallow 20 x 30 cm baking tin and line the base and sides with baking paper, leaving the paper hanging over the two long sides.

2 Place the butter, vanilla essence and sugar in a large bowl and cream with electric beaters until light and fluffy. Stir in the flour and mix until well combined.

3 Press the mixture firmly and evenly into the prepared tin and bake for 25 minutes, or until the base is cooked and a little browned. Cool slightly.

4 Place the extra butter, condensed milk and golden syrup in a saucepan and stir over low heat until the butter has melted. Increase the heat to medium, and stir constantly for 15–20 minutes, or until the mixture is thick and caramel-like. Add the macadamias and pour onto the biscuit base. Bake for 10 minutes, or until slightly browned. Cool in the tin. Cut in half lengthways, then into fingers.

Nutrition per piece: Fat 24 g; Protein 7 g; Carbohydrate 44 g; Dietary Fibre 1 g; Cholesterol 50.5 mg; 1715 kJ (410 cal)

Classic brownies (top), and Macadamia fingers

DATE CARAMEL SHORTCAKE

Prep time: 30 minutes + refrigeration
Cooking time: 50 minutes
Makes 12 pieces

125 g unsalted butter, softened
1/2 cup (125 g) caster sugar
1 teaspoon vanilla essence
1 egg
2 cups (250 g) plain flour
1 teaspoon baking powder
1 cup (175 g) roughly chopped seedless dates
1 tablespoon soft brown sugar
2 teaspoons cocoa powder
10 g unsalted butter, extra
icing sugar, to sprinkle

1 Preheat the oven to moderate 180°C (350°F/ Gas 4). Lightly grease a 18 x 27 cm shallow baking tin. Line with baking paper, leaving it hanging over the two long sides.
2 Beat the butter, sugar and vanilla with electric beaters until light and fluffy. Beat in the egg, then transfer to a bowl. Fold in the combined sifted flour and baking powder in batches with a metal spoon.
3 Press half the dough into the tin. Form the other half into a ball, cover and refrigerate for 30 minutes.
4 Place the dates, brown sugar, cocoa, extra butter and 1 cup (250 ml) water in a small saucepan. Bring to the boil, stirring, then reduce the heat and simmer, stirring, for 12–15 minutes, or until dates are soft and mushy and the water has been absorbed. Spread onto a plate and refrigerate to cool quickly.
5 Spread the filling over the pastry base with a metal spatula, then grate the remaining dough over the top. Bake for 35 minutes, or until light brown and crisp. Cool in the tin for 15 minutes then lift onto a wire rack. Sprinkle with icing sugar and cut into squares.

Nutrition per piece: Fat 10 g; Protein 3 g; Carbohydrate 37 g; Dietary Fibre 2 g; Cholesterol 43.5 mg; 1035 kJ (250 cal)

FIG AND CINNAMON SLICE

Prep time: 15 minutes
Cooking time: 55 minutes
Makes 15 small squares

1/2 cup (125 g) unsalted butter, softened
1/4 cup (55 g) soft brown sugar, firmly packed
1 teaspoon ground cinnamon
11/2 cups (185 g) plain flour
375 g dried figs
1 cinnamon stick
1/2 cup (125 g) caster sugar

1 Preheat the oven to moderate 180°C (350°F/ Gas 4). Lightly grease a 18 x 27 cm baking tin and line with baking paper, hanging over the two long sides.
2 Beat the butter, brown sugar and cinnamon until light and fluffy, then fold in the flour with a large metal spoon. Press the mixture evenly into the tin and bake for 25 minutes. Cool slightly.
3 Place the dried figs, cinnamon stick, sugar and 11/2 cups (375 ml) boiling water in a saucepan, mix together and bring to the boil. Reduce the heat and simmer for 20 minutes, or until the figs have softened and the water has reduced by a third. Remove the cinnamon stick and place the mixture in a food processor. Process in short bursts until smooth.
4 Pour onto the cooked base and bake for 10 minutes, or until set. Cool in the tin and when cold, lift out and cut into squares.

Nutrition per square: Fat 7.5 g; Protein 2.5 g; Carbohydrate 34.5 g; Dietary Fibre 4 g; Cholesterol 21 mg; 870 kJ (210 cal)

Date caramel shortcake (top), and Fig and cinnamon slice

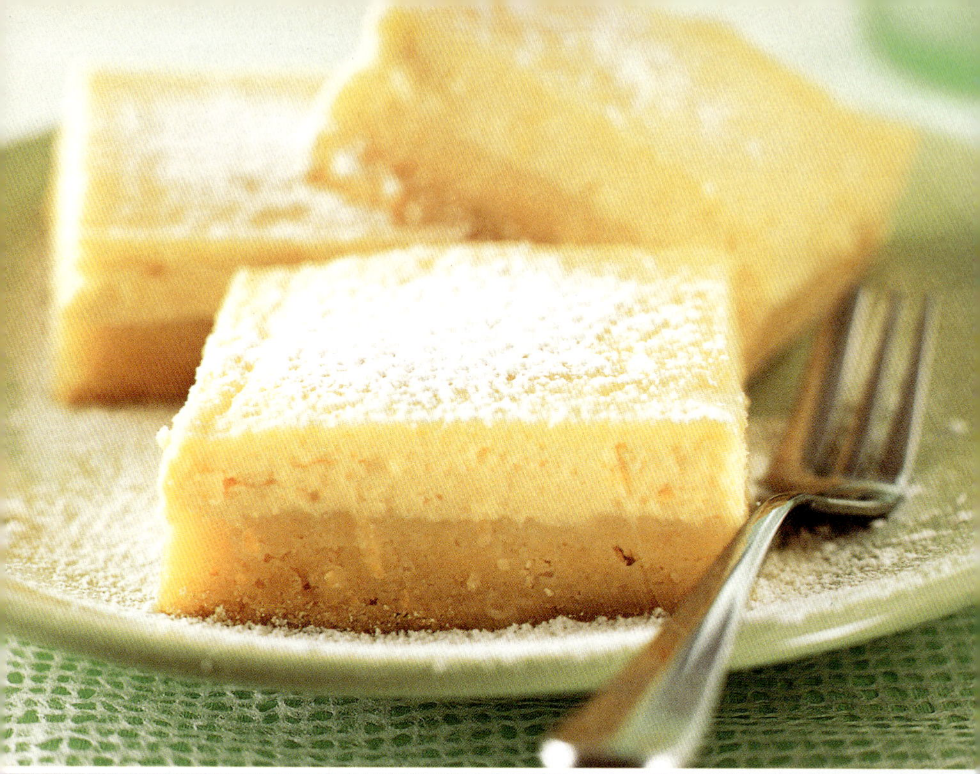
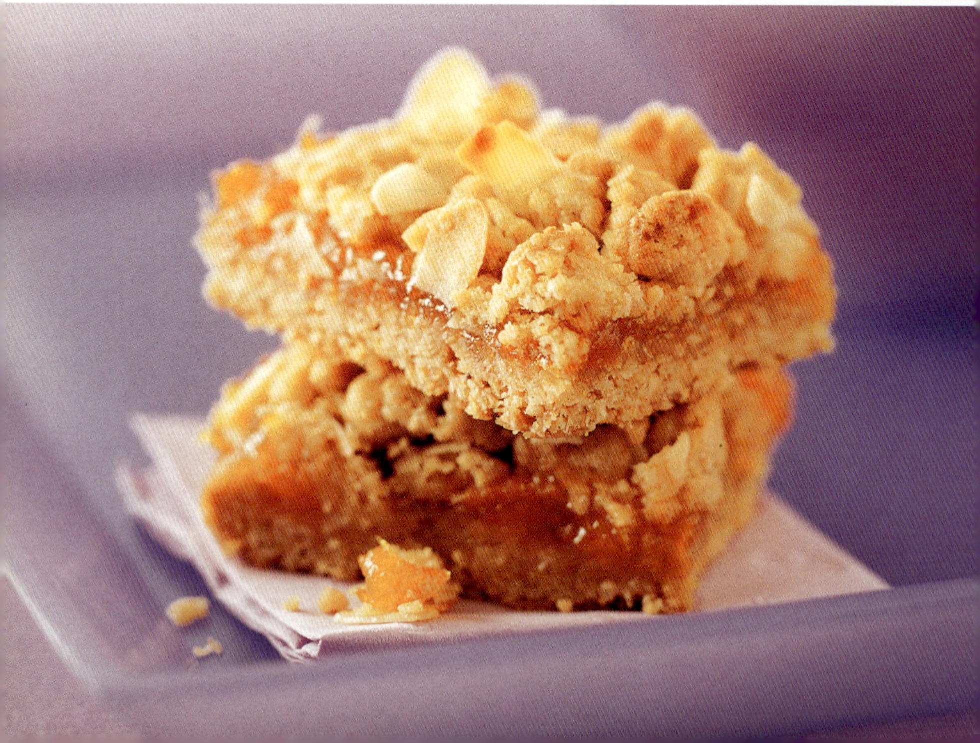

LEMON RICOTTA SLICE

Prep time: 15 minutes +
  2 hours refrigeration
Cooking time: 45 minutes
Makes 15 pieces

13/4 cups (220 g) plain flour
1 teaspoon baking powder
180 g unsalted butter,
  melted
210 g caster sugar
4 eggs
350 g ricotta cheese
200 ml cream
2 tablespoons lemon rind
3/4 cup (185 ml) lemon juice
icing sugar, for dusting

1 Preheat the oven to moderate 180°C (350°F/Gas 4). Lightly grease a 20 x 30 cm slice tin and line with baking paper, hanging over the two long sides.
2 Place the flour, baking powder, butter and 100 g of the sugar in a food processor and process in short bursts until the mixture comes together in a ball. Add 1 egg and process until combined.
3 Press the mixture into the tin. Bake for 15 minutes. Remove from the oven. Reduce the oven to slow 150°C (300°F/Gas 2).
4 Place the ricotta, cream, lemon rind and

Lemon ricotta slice (top), and Apricot crumble slice

juice, remaining sugar and remaining eggs in the cleaned food processor and combine for 1–2 seconds. Pour onto the pastry base and bake for 25–30 minutes— the slice will still have a slight wobble at this stage. Cool slightly, then refrigerate for 2 hours to firm. Cut into pieces. Dust with icing sugar and serve.

Nutrition per piece: Fat 20 g;
Protein 6 g; Carbohydrate 26 g;
Dietary Fibre 0.5 g; Cholesterol
107.5 mg; 1270 kJ (305 cal)

APRICOT CRUMBLE SLICE

Prep time: 20 minutes +
  10 minutes standing
Cooking time: 35 minutes
Makes 18 pieces

1 cup (150 g) chopped dried apricots
11/2 cups (185 g) plain flour
1 teaspoon baking powder
1 cup (185 g) soft brown sugar
2 cups (200 g) quick-cooking rolled oats
250 g unsalted butter, chilled and chopped
1 cup (315 g) apricot jam
1 teaspoon finely chopped lemon rind
1 teaspoon finely chopped orange rind
1/2 cup (45 g) flaked almonds

1 Preheat the oven to moderate 180°C (350°F/Gas 4). Grease a 20 x 30 cm baking tin and line with baking paper, hanging over the two long sides.
2 Place the apricots in a heatproof bowl, cover with 2 cups (500 ml) boiling water and leave for 10 minutes. Drain.
3 Sift the flour and baking powder into a large bowl. Add the sugar and oats and mix well. Rub the butter into the mixture with your fingers until it resembles coarse breadcrumbs. Reserve 11/2 cups of the crumble mixture to use as the topping.
4 Press the remaining crumble mixture into the prepared tin and bake for 15 minutes, then cool. Combine the apricots, apricot jam and citrus rinds and spread evenly over the cooled base. Add the flaked almonds to the reserved crumble mixture, combine well and lightly sprinkle over of the apricot mixture. Bake for 15–20 minutes, or until golden brown. Cool in the tin and cut into slices.

Nutrition per piece: Fat 14 g;
Protein 4 g; Carbohydrate 40 g;
Dietary Fibre 2.5 g; Cholesterol
35 mg; 1225 kJ (295 cal)

VANILLA SLICE

Prep time: 40 minutes
Cooking time: 15 minutes
Makes 9 pieces

500 g ready-made puff
pastry (or see Note)
1 cup (250 g) caster sugar
3/4 cup (90 g) cornflour
1/2 cup (60 g) custard
powder
1 litre cream
60 g unsalted butter, cubed
2 teaspoons vanilla essence
3 egg yolks

Icing
1 1/2 cups (185 g) icing sugar
1/4 cup (60 g) passionfruit
pulp
15 g unsalted butter, melted

1 Preheat the oven to
hot 210°C (415°F/
Gas 6–7). Lightly grease
two baking trays with
oil. Line the base and
sides of a shallow 23 cm
square cake tin with foil,
leaving the foil hanging
over two opposite sides.
2 Divide the pastry in
half, roll each piece to
a 25 cm square about
3 mm thick and place
each on a baking tray.
Prick all over with a fork
and bake for 8 minutes,
or until golden. Trim
each pastry sheet to a
23 cm square. Place one
sheet top-side-down in
the cake tin.
3 Combine the sugar,
cornflour and custard
powder in a saucepan.

Stir in the cream until
smooth. Stir constantly
over medium heat for
2 minutes, or until it
boils and thickens. Add
the butter and essence
and stir until smooth.
Remove from the heat
and immediately whisk
in the egg yolks until
combined. Spread the
custard over the pastry
in the tin, then cover
with the other pastry
sheet, top-side-down.
Cool completely.
4 To make the icing,
combine the icing sugar,
passionfruit pulp and
butter in a bowl, and stir
until smooth.
5 Lift the slice out of
the tin, using the foil as
handles and spread the
icing over the top. Leave
to set before cutting
with a serrated knife.

Nutrition per piece: Fat 67 g;
Protein 7 g; Carbohydrate 87 g;
Dietary Fibre 1.5 g; Cholesterol
240 mg; 4005 kJ (955 cal)

Note: If you'd like to make your
own pastry, this recipe will make
about 500 g. Sift 2 cups (250 g)
plain flour and 1/2 teaspoon salt
onto a work surface and make
a well in the centre. Add 30 g
melted unsalted butter and
2/3 cup (170 ml) chilled water
and blend with your fingertips,
gradually drawing in the flour until
it resembles a crumb mixture—if
it's a little dry, add extra drops of
water before bringing it together
to form a dough. Cut the dough
with a pastry scraper, using a
downward cutting action, then

turn the dough and repeat in the
opposite direction. Bring together
to form a soft ball. Score a cross
in the top, cover in plastic wrap
and chill for 15–20 minutes.
Pound 170–220 g unsalted
butter between two sheets of
baking paper with a rolling pin,
then roll into a 10 cm square—it
must be the same consistency
as the dough or they will not roll
out the same amount and the
layers will not be even. If the
butter is too soft, it will squeeze
out of the sides. Too hard and it
will break through the dough and
disturb the layers. Roll the pastry
out on a well-floured surface, to
form a cross, leaving the centre
slightly thicker than the arms.
Place the butter in the centre of
the cross and fold over each arm
to make a parcel. Turn the dough
so that it looks like a book with
the hinge side to the left. Tap and
roll out the dough to form a neat
15 x 45 cm rectangle—square
off the corners. Fold the dough
like a letter: the top third down
and the bottom third up, to form
a square, brushing off any
excess flour between the layers.
Turn the dough 90° to bring the
hinge side to your left and press
the seam sides down with the
rolling pin to seal. Re-roll and fold
as before to complete two turns.
Cover in plastic wrap and chill
again for at least 30 minutes.
Re-roll and fold two more times
and chill. Re-roll a final two times
to complete six turns in total. (In
hot weather, chill for 30 minutes
between each turn, rather than
after a double turn.) Refrigerate
until ready to use.

Vanilla slice

GINGER PANFORTE SLICE

Prep time: 20 minutes
Cooking time: 40 minutes
Makes 20 pieces

1/3 cup (40 g) plain flour
1 tablespoon cocoa powder
1 teaspoon ground ginger
1/2 teaspoon ground
  cardamom
1 teaspoon ground
  cinnamon
125 g dried figs, chopped
50 g glacé ginger, chopped
50 g glacé pineapple,
  chopped
50 g glacé apricots, chopped
50 chopped mixed peel
175 g blanched almonds,
  toasted
1/3 cup (90 g) caster sugar
1/4 cup (90 g) honey

1 Preheat the oven to moderate 160°C (315°F/ Gas 2-3). Lightly grease a 7 x 25 cm shallow bar tin and line with baking paper, hanging over at the two short ends.
2 Sift the flour, cocoa, ginger and spices into a large bowl. Add the fruit and almonds.
3 Heat the sugar, honey and 2 teaspoons water in a small saucepan over low heat, stirring until melted and it just comes to the boil. Pour onto the dry ingredients and mix well. Press the

Ginger panforte slice (top), and Poppy seed slice

mixture into the tin and bake for 35–40 minutes, or until just firm. Cool in the tin, then chill until firm. Cut into thin slices.

Nutrition per piece: Fat 5 g; Protein 3 g; Carbohydrate 21 g; Dietary Fibre 2 g; Cholesterol 0 mg; 555 kJ (130 cal)

POPPY SEED SLICE

Prep time: 35 minutes +
  15 minutes refrigeration +
  10 minutes soaking
Cooking time: 40 minutes
Makes 14 pieces

135 g plain flour
75 g unsalted butter, chilled
  and chopped
1/4 cup (60 g) caster sugar
1 egg yolk
1/4 cup (40 g) poppy seeds
2 tablespoons milk, warmed
125 g unsalted butter, extra
1/3 cup (90 g) caster sugar,
  extra
1 teaspoon finely grated
  lemon rind
1 egg
3/4 cup (90 g) plain flour,
  extra, sifted
1 cup (125 g) icing sugar
1/2 teaspoon finely grated
  lemon rind, extra
1 tablespoon lemon juice

1 Preheat the oven to moderate 180°C (350°F/ Gas 4). Grease a 11 x 35 cm loose-based flan tin. Sift the flour into a bowl and rub in the butter with your fingers

until it looks like fine breadcrumbs. Stir in the sugar. Make a well in the centre and add 2–3 teaspoons water and the egg yolk. Mix with a flat-bladed knife, using a cutting action until it comes together in beads. Press into a ball and flatten slightly. Wrap in plastic wrap and chill for 15 minutes.
2 Roll out the dough to fit the base and sides of the tin. Trim the edges. Line with baking paper and pour in baking beads or uncooked rice. Bake for 10 minutes, then remove the paper and beads and bake for 5 minutes, or until the pastry is dry. Cool.
3 Soak the poppy seeds in the milk for 10 minutes. Beat the extra butter and sugar and the rind until light and fluffy. Beat in the egg and stir in the poppy seed mixture and extra flour. Spread over the pastry and bake for 25 minutes, or until light brown and cooked through. Cool in the tin until just warm.
4 Combine the icing sugar, extra rind and enough juice to form a paste. Spread over the slice and cool.

Nutrition per piece: Fat 14 g; Protein 3 g; Carbohydrate 32 g; Dietary Fibre 1 g; Cholesterol 62 mg; 1100 kJ (260 cal)

STRAWBERRY AND MASCARPONE SLICE

Prep time: 25 minutes +
    3 hours refrigeration
Cooking time: 25 minutes
Makes 24 pieces

175 g unsalted butter,
    softened
70 g caster sugar
1 egg yolk
2 cups (250 g) plain flour,
    sifted
300 g mascarpone
1/2 cup (60 g) icing sugar,
    sifted
1 tablespoon lemon juice
300 g strawberries, cut into
    quarters
50 g dark chocolate

1 Preheat the oven to moderate 180°C (350°F/ Gas 4). Lightly grease a 20 x 30 cm shallow baking tin and line with baking paper, leaving it hanging over the two long sides.
2 Beat the butter and sugar with electric beaters until light and fluffy. Add the egg yolk and beat well. Fold in the sifted flour until well combined. Press firmly into the prepared tray and prick all over with a fork. Bake for 25 minutes, or until light brown. Cool completely.
3 Beat the mascarpone, icing sugar and juice with a wooden spoon until smooth. Stir in the strawberries. Spoon over the base and refrigerate for 3 hours, or until firm.
4 Chop the chocolate into small even-sized pieces and place in a heatproof bowl. Bring a saucepan of water to the boil, then remove from the heat. Sit the bowl over the pan—ensure the bowl doesn't touch the water. Stand, stirring occasionally, until the chocolate has melted. Drizzle over the slice, then cut into pieces.

Nutrition per piece: Fat 11 g; Protein 3 g; Carbohydrate 15 g; Dietary Fibre 0.5 g; Cholesterol 38 mg; 705 kJ (170 cal)

CHOCOLATE TRUFFLE MACAROON SLICE

Prep time: 15 minutes +
    3 hours refrigeration
Cooking time: 20 minutes
Makes 24 pieces

3 egg whites
3/4 cup (185 g) caster sugar
2 cups (180 g) desiccated
    coconut
250 g dark chocolate
300 ml cream
1 tablespoon cocoa powder

1 Preheat the oven to moderate 180°C (350°F/ Gas 4). Lightly grease a 20 x 30 cm shallow baking tin and line with baking paper, leaving it hanging over the two long sides.
2 Beat the egg whites in a clean, dry bowl until soft peaks form. Slowly add the sugar, beating well after each addition until stiff and glossy. Fold in the coconut. Spread into the tin and bake for 20 minutes, or until light brown. While still warm, press down lightly but firmly with a palette knife. Cool completely.
3 Chop the chocolate into small even-sized pieces and place in a heatproof bowl. Bring a saucepan of water to the boil, then remove from the heat. Sit the bowl over the pan—ensure the bowl doesn't touch the water. Stand, stirring occasionally, until the chocolate has melted. Cool slightly.
4 Beat the cream until thick. Gently fold in the chocolate until well combined—do not overmix or it will curdle. Spread evenly over the base and refrigerate for 3 hours, or until set. Lift from the tin and dust with the cocoa.

Nutrition per piece: Fat 13 g; Protein 2 g; Carbohydrate 15 g; Dietary Fibre 1 g; Cholesterol 17 mg; 760 kJ (180 cal)

Strawberry and mascarpone slice (top), and Chocolate truffle macaroon slice

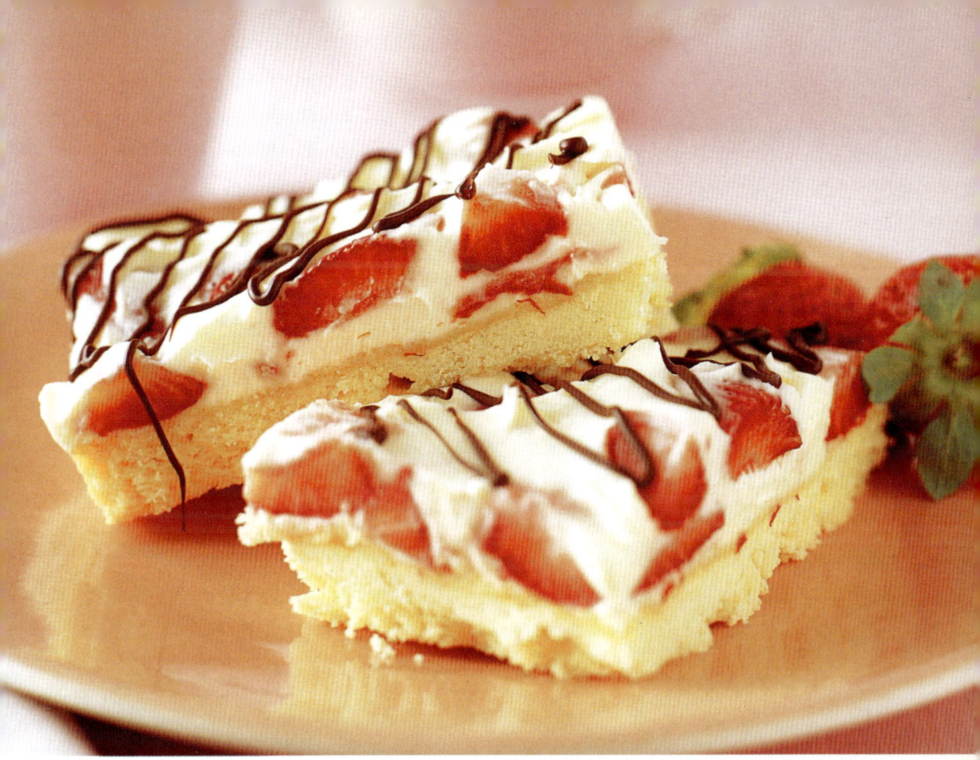

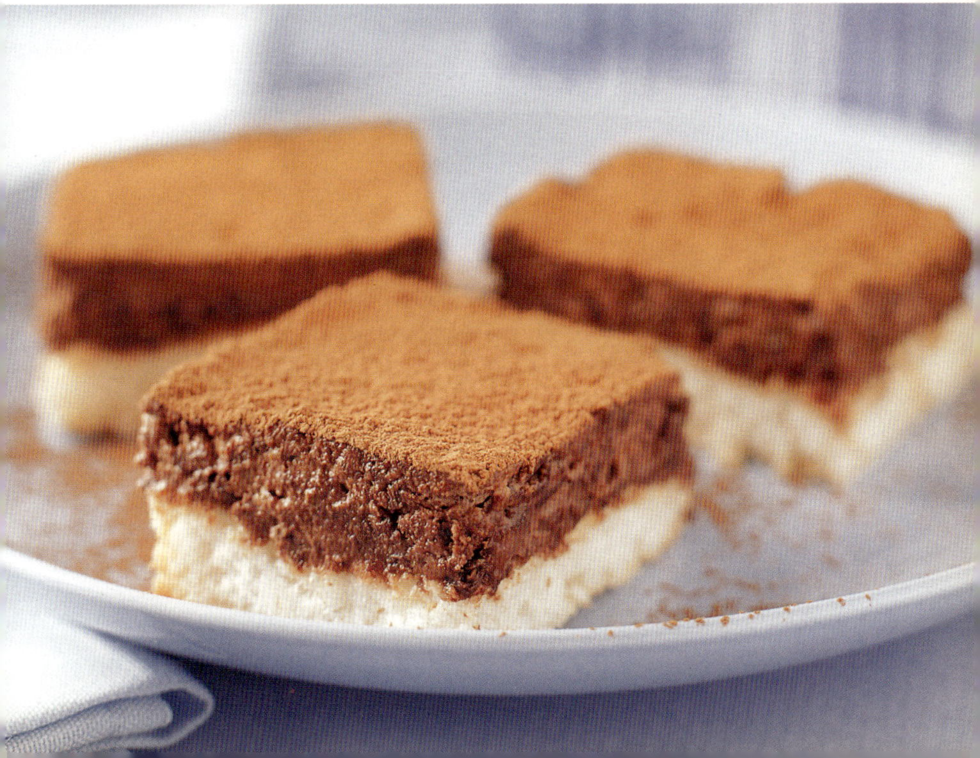

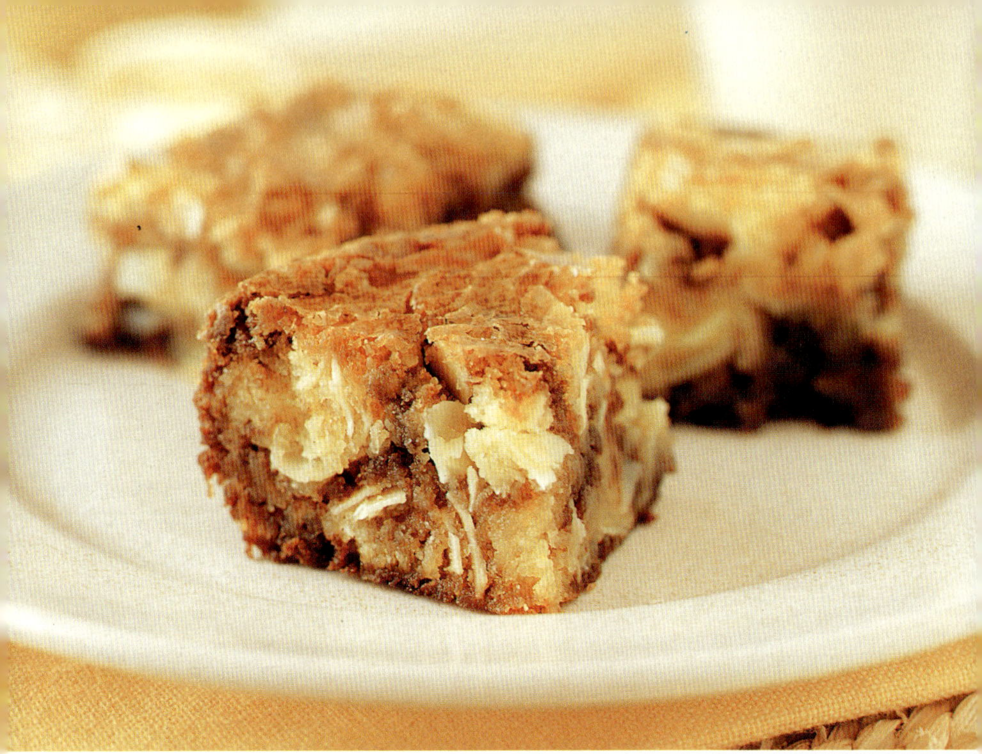

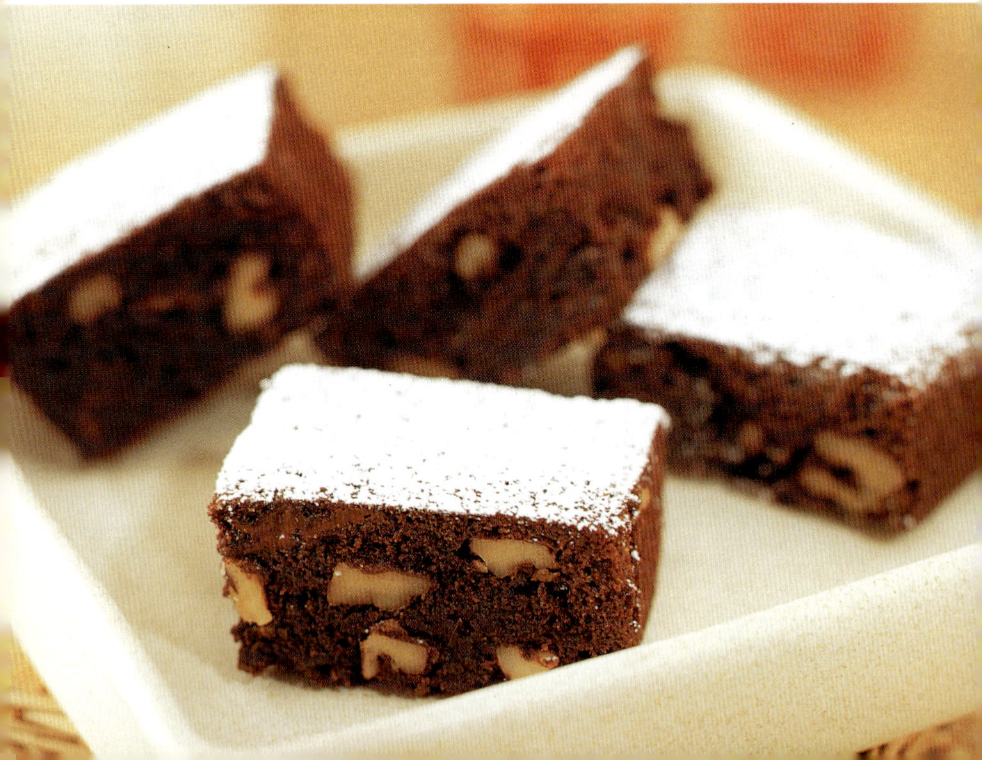

CHOCOLATE AND AMARETTO BROWNIES

Prep time: 15 minutes
Cooking time: 35 minutes
Makes 9 pieces

Dark chocolate mixture
60 g unsalted butter
90 g dark chocolate
1/2 cup (125 g) caster sugar
1 teaspoon vanilla essence
1 egg, lightly beaten
1/2 cup (60 g) plain flour

Amaretto mixture
60 g unsalted butter
90 g white chocolate
1/2 cup (125 g) caster sugar
2 tablespoons Amaretto
1 egg, lightly beaten
1/2 cup (45 g) flaked
  almonds
3/4 cup (90 g) plain flour,
  sifted

1 Preheat the oven to moderate 180°C (350°F/ Gas 4). Lightly grease a 17 cm square tin and line with baking paper, hanging over two sides.
2 To make the dark chocolate mixture, chop the butter and chocolate into small even-sized pieces and place in a small heatproof bowl. Bring a saucepan of water to the boil and remove from the heat. Sit the bowl over the

pan—ensure it doesn't touch the water. Stand, stirring occasionally, until just melted. Beat the sugar, vanilla and egg with a wooden spoon until combined. Stir in the chocolate mixture. Add the flour and stir until just combined—do not overmix.
3 To make the Amaretto mixture, chop the butter and white chocolate and place in a small heatproof bowl. Bring a saucepan of water to the boil and remove from the heat. Sit the bowl over the pan—ensure the bowl doesn't touch the water. Stand, stirring occasionally, until the chocolate and butter have just melted. Beat the sugar, Amaretto and egg until combined. Stir in the white chocolate mixture, then add the almonds and flour and stir until just combined— do not overmix.
4 Drop large spoonfuls of the two mixtures alternately, in a single layer in the tin. Gently swirl together and smooth the surface. Bake for 35 minutes, or until firm. Cool in the tin, then on a wire rack. Cut into squares.

Nutrition per piece: Fat 21 g;
Protein 6 g; Carbohydrate 54 g;
Dietary Fibre 1 g; Cholesterol
75.5 mg; 1800 kJ (433 cal)

WALNUT BROWNIES

Prep time: 15 minutes
Cooking time: 25 minutes
Makes 24 pieces

2/3 cup (85 g) self-raising
  flour
2/3 cup (85 g) cocoa powder
1 cup (250 g) caster sugar
330 g unsalted butter, melted
4 eggs, lightly beaten
1 teaspoon vanilla essence
250 g dark choc bits
1 cup (125 g) walnut pieces
icing sugar, for dusting

1 Preheat the oven to moderate 180°C (350°F/ Gas 4). Grease a 20 x 30 cm shallow baking tin and line with baking paper, leaving it hanging over the two long sides.
2 Sift together the flour and cocoa, then add the sugar. Make a well in the centre, then add the butter, eggs and vanilla and beat until smooth. Fold in the choc bits and nuts. Spoon into the baking tin and smooth the surface. Bake for 25 minutes, or until a skewer comes out clean. Leave in the tin for 10 minutes, then turn onto a wire rack to cool. Dust with icing sugar.

Nutrition per piece: Fat 19.5 g;
Protein 4 g; Carbohydrate 21 g;
Dietary Fibre 1 g; Cholesterol
64.5 mg; 1105 kJ (265 cal)

Chocolate and Amaretto
brownies (top), and
Walnut brownies

PEAR AND WALNUT SLICE

Prep time: 15 minutes
Cooking time: 40 minutes
Makes 18 pieces

1 1/2 cups (185 g) plain flour
1 teaspoon baking powder
1/2 teaspoon ground ginger
1 teaspoon ground
    cinnamon
3 eggs
1 1/2 cups (280 g) soft
    brown sugar
1 teaspoon brandy
1 teaspoon vanilla essence
1 teaspoon finely grated
    orange rind
1 cup (25 g) walnut pieces
2 medium pears, peeled,
    cored and chopped
1/2 cup (80 g) raisins,
    chopped
icing sugar, for dusting

1 Preheat the oven to moderate 180°C (350°F/ Gas 4). Lightly grease a 20 x 30 cm shallow tin and line with baking paper, hanging over the two long sides.
2 Sift together the flour, baking powder, ginger and cinnamon. Beat the eggs, sugar, brandy and vanilla in a large bowl for 3 minutes, or until pale and foamy, then add the orange rind. Gently fold the dry ingredients into the egg mixture with a large metal spoon. Add the walnuts, pears and raisins and gently mix.

3 Spread the mixture into the tin and bake for 35–40 minutes, or until a skewer inserted into the centre comes out clean. Cool in the tin. Slice and serve dusted with icing sugar.

Nutrition per piece: Fat 2 g; Protein 3 g; Carbohydrate 29 g; Dietary Fibre 1 g; Cholesterol 30 mg; 580 kJ (140 cal)

APPLE SHORTCAKE

Prep time: 30 minutes +
    30 minutes chilling
Cooking time: 45 minutes
Makes 9 pieces

2 cups (250 g) plain flour
1 teaspoon baking powder
125 g unsalted butter,
    chilled and chopped
1/4 cup (60 g) caster sugar
1 egg, lightly beaten
1 tablespoon cold milk
4 small red apples, peeled,
    quartered and cored
1 teaspoon ground
    cinnamon
1 tablespoon milk, extra
2 tablespoons caster sugar,
    extra
demerara sugar, to sprinkle

1 Preheat the oven to moderate 180°C (350°F/ Gas 4). Lightly grease a baking tray and line with baking paper, hanging over the two long sides.
2 Sift the flour and baking powder into a large bowl, add the butter and rub with your fingertips until the mixture resembles fine breadcrumbs. Stir in the sugar.
3 Make a well in the centre and add the combined egg and milk. Mix with a flat-bladed knife using a cutting action until the mixture comes together in beads. Gently gather together and lift out onto a lightly floured work surface. Press together into a ball, flatten slightly, wrap in plastic wrap and chill for 20–30 minutes.
4 Halve the dough— keep one half in the refrigerator and roll the other half into an even 20 cm square. Place on the baking tray. Cut the apple quarters into thin slices and arrange in rows, to form a double layer of apples over the pastry. Sprinkle with the cinnamon and extra caster sugar.
6 Roll the remaining pastry into a 20 cm square and place over the apple. Brush with extra milk and sprinkle with the demerara sugar. Bake for 40–45 minutes, or until crisp and golden.

Nutrition per piece: Fat 12.5 g; Protein 4 g; Carbohydrate 36 g; Dietary Fibre 2 g; Cholesterol 55.5 mg; 1125 kJ (270 cal)

Pear and walnut slice (top), and Apple shortcake

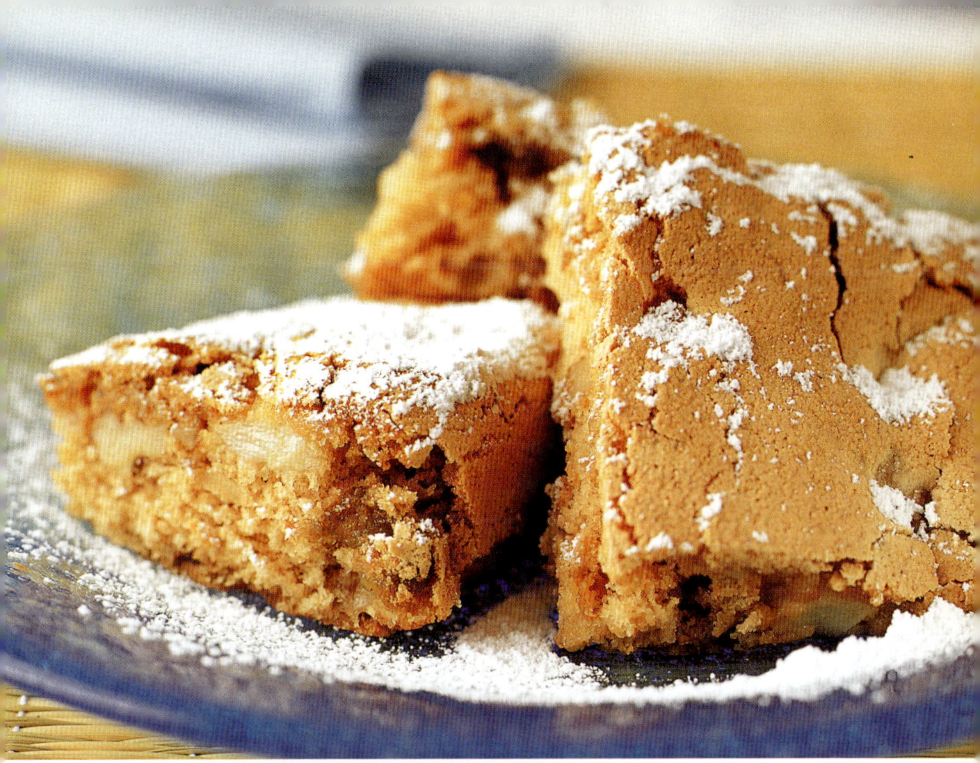

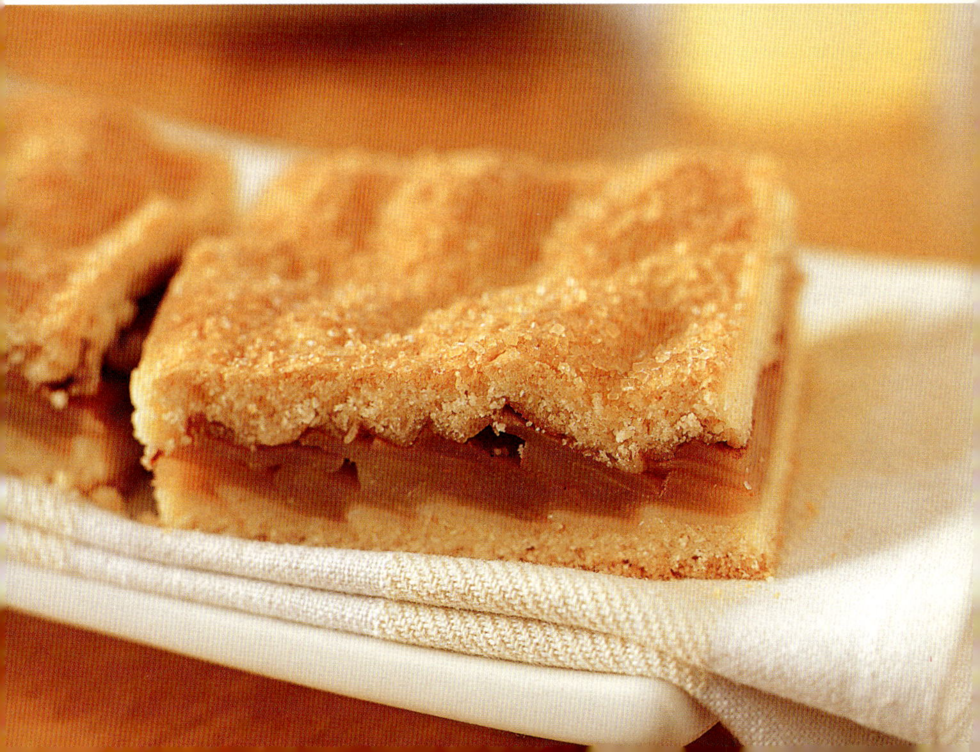

SNICKERDOODLE SLICE

Prep time: 15 minutes
Cooking time: 30 minutes
Makes 20 pieces

2 cups (250 g) plain flour
1 cup (250 g) caster sugar
1 tablespoon ground
  cinnamon
2 teaspoons baking powder
2 eggs
1 cup (250 ml) milk
125 g unsalted butter,
  melted
3 tablespoons sugar
3 teaspoons ground
  cinnamon, extra

1 Preheat the oven to moderate 180°C (350°F/Gas 4). Lightly grease a 20 x 30 cm baking tin and line with baking paper, hanging over the two long sides.
2 Sift together the flour, caster sugar, cinnamon and baking powder and make a well in the centre. In a small bowl, whisk together the eggs and milk. Pour into the flour and mix with a metal spoon to roughly combine. Fold in the butter until smooth—do not overmix. Spoon half the mixture into the tin and level the surface.
3 Combine the sugar and extra cinnamon, and sprinkle two-thirds over

Snickerdoodle slice (top), and No-bake chocolate slice

the mixture in the tin. Gently spoon the remaining mixture over the top, then sprinkle the remaining cinnamon sugar over the surface. Bake for 25–30 minutes, or until firm. Cool in the tin for 20 minutes, then lift onto a wire rack to cool.

Nutrition per piece: Fat 6.5 g; Protein 3 g; Carbohydrate 25 g; Dietary Fibre 0.5 g; Cholesterol 35.5 mg; 680 kJ (160 cal)

NO-BAKE CHOCOLATE SLICE

Prep time: 15 minutes +
  overnight refrigeration
Cooking time: Nil
Makes 18 pieces

100 g shortbread biscuits,
  roughly crushed
120 g pistachios, shelled
150 g hazelnuts, toasted
  and skinned
100 g glacé cherries,
  roughly chopped
300 g good-quality dark
  (not bitter) chocolate
200 g unsalted butter
1 teaspoon instant coffee
  powder
2 eggs, lightly beaten

1 Lightly grease a 18 x 27 cm baking tin and line with baking paper, hanging over the two long sides.
2 Combine the crushed biscuits, pistachios,

90 g hazelnuts, and half the cherries.
3 Chop the chocolate and butter into small even-sized pieces and place in a heatproof bowl. Bring a saucepan of water to the boil and remove from the heat. Sit the bowl over the pan—ensure the bowl doesn't touch the water. Allow to stand, stirring occasionally, until the chocolate and butter have melted. Remove the bowl from the pan and when the mixture has cooled slightly, mix in the coffee and eggs. Pour over the nut mixture and mix well.
4 Pour the slice mixture into the tin and pat down well. Roughly chop the remaining hazelnuts and sprinkle over the top with the remaining cherries. Refrigerate overnight.
5 Remove from the tin and trim the edges of the slice before cutting into pieces. Keep in the refrigerator.

Nutrition per piece: Fat 24.5 g; Protein 5 g; Carbohydrate 19 g; Dietary Fibre 2 g; Cholesterol 49.5 mg; 1285 kJ (305 cal)

Note: Toast the hazelnuts in a moderate 180°C (350°F/Gas 4) oven for 5–10 minutes, or until lightly golden. Tip the nuts onto a clean tea towel and rub gently to remove the skins.

HAZELNUT MERINGUE AND CHOCOLATE LAYER SLICE

Prep time: 30 minutes +
1 hour refrigeration
Cooking time: 30 minutes
Makes 18 pieces

110 g hazelnuts, lightly
toasted and skinned
1/4 cup (30 g) cornflour
1/3 cup (40 g) icing sugar
5 egg whites
200 g caster sugar
cocoa powder, for dusting

Ganache
250 g bitter chocolate
1/2 cup (125 ml) cream
2 tablespoons Frangelico

1 Preheat the oven to warm 170°C (325°F/ Gas 3). Lightly grease two 38 x 26 cm baking trays and line with baking paper.
2 Place the hazelnuts, cornflour and icing sugar in a food processor and chop in short bursts until the nuts are the size of coarse breadcrumbs.
3 Beat the egg whites in a clean, dry bowl with electric beaters until soft peaks form. Gradually add the sugar and beat until thick and glossy. Lightly fold the egg white into the hazelnut mixture. Divide the mixture evenly between the two trays, spread out and smooth the surface.

4 Bake for 30 minutes, or until light golden. Trim the edges and cut a 26 cm square from both meringues, reserving the shorter pieces. Allow to cool completely.
5 To make the ganache, chop the chocolate into small even-sized pieces and put in a small heatproof bowl with the cream and Frangelico. Bring a saucepan of water to the boil and remove from the heat. Sit the bowl over the pan, making sure the bowl does not touch the water. Allow to stand, stirring occasionally, until the chocolate has just melted. Stir until smooth, then cover the surface with plastic wrap and leave to cool completely, stirring occasionally.
6 Line a 26 cm square tin with baking paper and leave the paper hanging over all sides. Line with one square of meringue and carefully smooth half the ganache over the top. Lay the smaller pieces of meringue side-by-side over the ganache, then smooth the remaining ganache over the top. Place the remaining meringue square on top, press gently and then refrigerate for 1 hour. Dust with the cocoa and cut into thin rectangles with a serrated knife.

Nutrition per piece: Fat 10.5 g;
Protein 3 g; Carbohydrate 26 g;
Dietary Fibre 1 g; Cholesterol
9.5 mg; 865 kJ (205 cal)

Note: Toast the hazelnuts in a moderate 180°C (350°F/Gas 4) oven for 5–10 minutes, or until lightly golden. Tip the nuts onto a clean tea towel and rub gently to remove the skins.

Don't worry if the pieces of meringue break up a little, the ganache will adhere the pieces when set.

Hazelnut meringue and chocolate layer slice

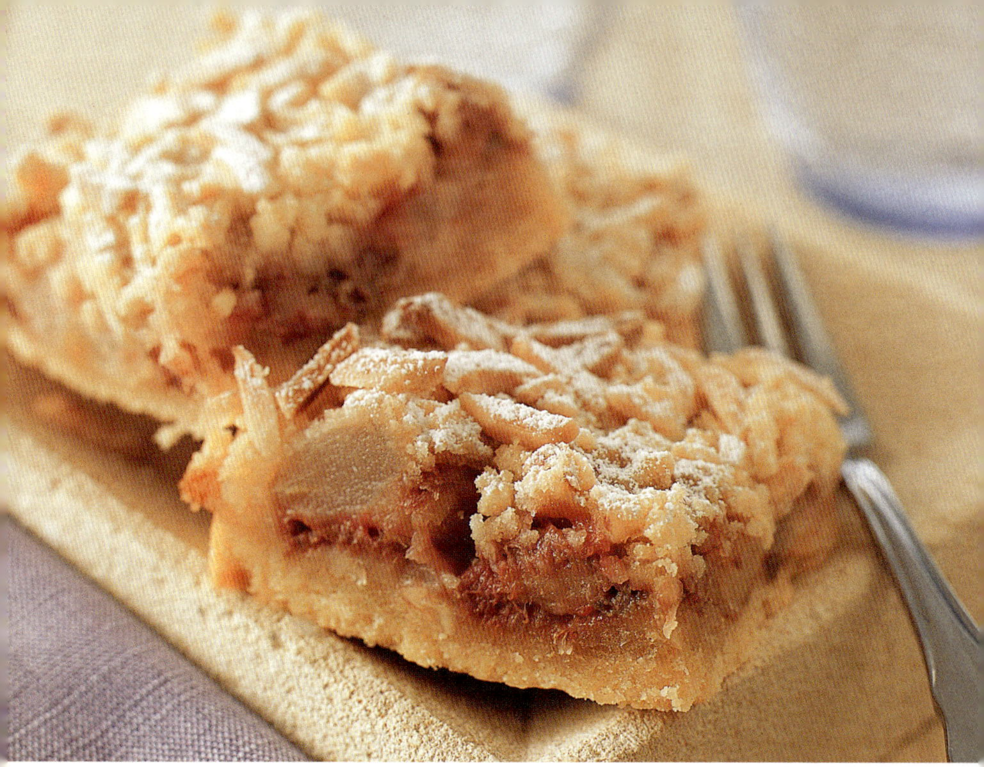

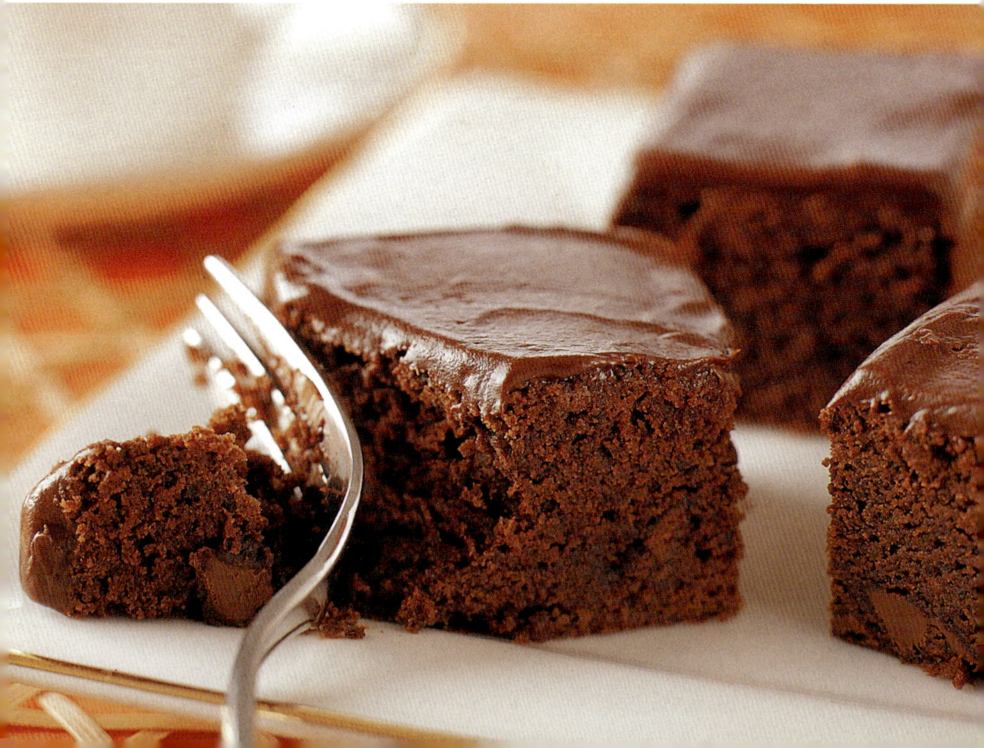

RHUBARB AND APPLE CRUMBLE SLICE

Prep time: 20 minutes
Cooking time: 1 hour
Makes 12 pieces

2 1/2 cups (310 g) plain flour
270 g unsalted butter
80 g caster sugar
1 egg yolk
200 g slivered almonds
450 g can pie apple
540 g can rhubarb, drained
1 teaspoon grated lemon
 rind
icing sugar, for dusting

1 Preheat the oven to moderate 180°C (350°F/ Gas 4). Lightly grease a 20 x 30 cm baking tin and line with baking paper, hanging over the two long sides.
2 Put 1 1/2 cups (185 g) flour, 145 g butter and 25 g caster sugar in a food processor and mix in short bursts until the mixture resemble fine crumbs. Add the egg yolk and 2 tablespoons cold water and mix in short bursts to combine (it will not form a ball like pastry). Press into the tin and bake for 15 minutes. Cool.
3 Place the remaining flour, butter and sugar in the food processor with

Rhubarb and apple crumble slice (top), and Mocha brownies

150 g almonds and mix in short bursts until the almonds are just chopped but not too fine. Set aside 1 cup mixture.
4 Fold the remaining crumb mixture, the apple, rhubarb and lemon rind together.
5 Cover the base with the fruit, sprinkle with the reserved crumble, then with the remaining slivered almonds. Bake for 40 minutes. Cool completely before cutting into slices and dusting with icing sugar.

Nutrition per piece: Fat 29 g; Protein 7 g; Carbohydrate 35 g; Dietary Fibre 4 g; Cholesterol 71.5 mg; 1770 kJ (425 cal)

MOCHA BROWNIES

Prep time: 15 minutes
Cooking time: 30 minutes
Makes 24 pieces

1 1/2 cups (185 g) plain flour
2/3 cup (85 g) cocoa powder
1 1/2 tablespoons instant
 coffee powder
2 cups (500 g) caster sugar
300 g unsalted butter, melted
4 eggs, lightly beaten
1 teaspoon vanilla essence
1 cup (205 g) dark choc bits
2 teaspoons finely grated
 orange rind
1/2 cup (125 ml) cream
250 g dark chocolate,
 chopped
2 tablespoons Kahlua,
 optional

1 Preheat the oven to moderate 180°C (350°F/ Gas 4). Lightly grease a 20 x 30 cm baking tin and line with baking paper, hanging over the two long sides.
2 Sift together the flour, cocoa and 2 teaspoons coffee powder. Stir in the sugar. Make a well in the centre and add the butter, eggs and vanilla and beat until smooth. Fold through the choc bits and orange rind.
3 Spread into the tin and bake for 30 minutes, or until a skewer comes out clean. Cool in the tin for 10 minutes, then cool on a wire rack.
4 Place the cream, dark chocolate, Kahlua and remaining coffee powder in a small heatproof bowl. Bring a saucepan of water to the boil, then remove the pan from the heat. Sit the bowl over the pan— ensure it doesn't touch the water. Stand, stirring occasionally, until the chocolate has melted and combined. Cool slightly and spread over the brownies.

Nutrition per piece: Fat 19.5 g; Protein 4 g; Carbohydrate 40 g; Dietary Fibre 1 g; Cholesterol 69 mg; 1450 kJ (345 cal)

BERRY AND APPLE SLICE

Prep time: 15 minutes
Cooking time: 40 minutes
Makes 12 pieces

150 g unsalted butter
11/3 cups (320 g) caster
  sugar
2 eggs, lightly beaten
2 cups (250 g) self-raising
  flour, sifted
2/3 cup (160 ml) buttermilk
1 teaspoon vanilla essence
2 large apples
150 g blueberries
150 g blackberries
icing sugar, for dusting

1 Preheat the oven to moderate 180°C (350°F/ Gas 4). Lightly grease a 30 x 20 cm shallow baking tin and line with baking paper, leaving it hanging over the two long sides.
2 Beat the butter and sugar with electric beaters until light and fluffy. Add the egg gradually, beating well after each addition. Stir in the flour and buttermilk alternately and mix until smooth. Stir through the vanilla. Spread a 5 mm layer of mixture over the base of the tin.
3 Peel, quarter and core the apples. Cut into very thin slices and arrange on the mixture. Spoon the remaining mixture over the apple and smooth the surface. Scatter with the berries. Bake on the middle rack for 40 minutes, or until cooked and golden.
4 Cool in the tin for 30 minutes before lifting onto a wire rack. When completely cooled, dust with icing sugar and cut into squares.

Nutrition per piece: Fat 12 g; Protein 4 g; Carbohydrate 49 g; Dietary Fibre 2.5 g; Cholesterol 62.5 mg; 1305 kJ (310 cal)

CHOCOLATE CARAMEL SLICE

Prep time: 20 minutes +
  30 minutes refrigeration
Cooking time: 15 minutes
Makes 24 triangles

200 g plain chocolate
  biscuits, crushed
100 g unsalted butter,
  melted
2 tablespoons desiccated
  coconut
125 g unsalted butter, extra
400 ml can sweetened
  condensed milk
1/3 cup (90 g) caster sugar
3 tablespoons maple syrup
250 g dark chocolate
2 teaspoons oil

1 Grease a 30 x 20 cm shallow baking tin and line with baking paper, leaving it hanging over the two long sides.
2 Combine the biscuit, melted butter and coconut in a bowl, then press evenly into the tin and smooth the surface.
3 Combine the butter, condensed milk, sugar and maple syrup in a small saucepan. Stir over low heat for 15 minutes, or until the sugar has dissolved and the mixture is smooth, thick and lightly coloured. Remove from the heat and cool slightly. Pour over the biscuit base and smooth the surface. Refrigerate for about 30 minutes, or until firm.
4 Chop the chocolate into small even-sized pieces and place in a heatproof bowl. Bring a saucepan of water to the boil and remove from the heat. Sit the bowl over the saucepan, making sure the bowl doesn't touch the water. Allow to stand, stirring occasionally, until the chocolate has melted. Add the oil and stir until smooth. Spread over the caramel and leave until partially set before marking into 24 triangles. Refrigerate until firm. Cut into triangles before serving. Store up to 2 days in an airtight container.

Nutrition per triangle: Fat 14 g; Protein 3 g; Carbohydrate 31 g; Dietary Fibre 0.5 g; Cholesterol 29 mg; 1055 kJ (250 cal)

Berry and apple slice (top), and Chocolate caramel slice

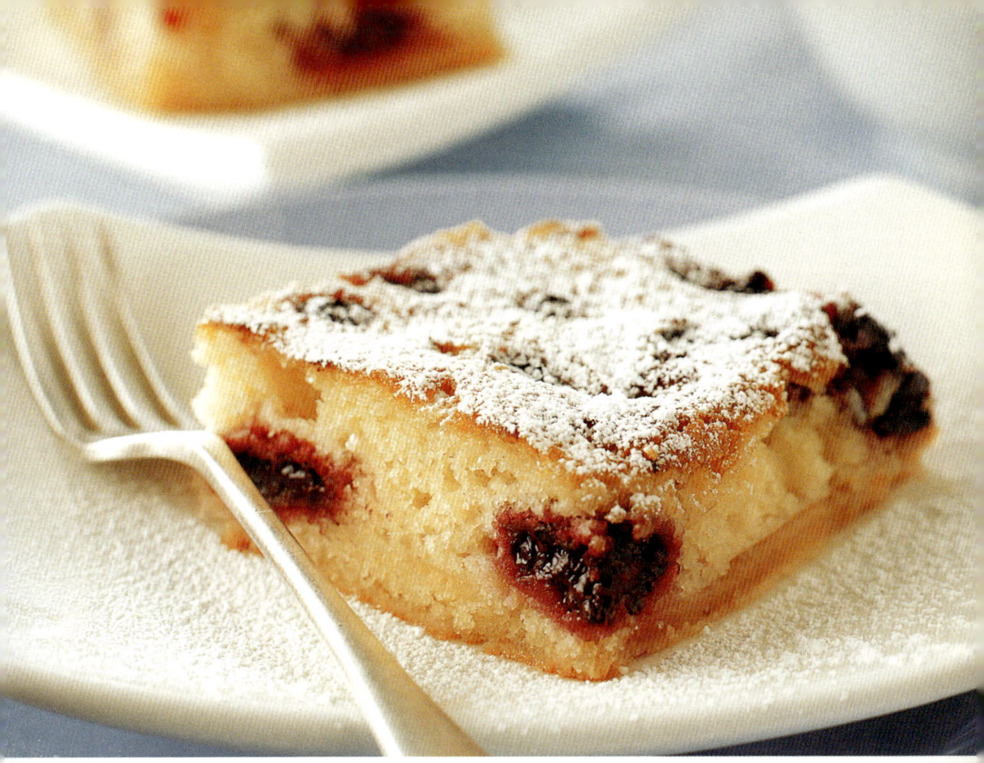

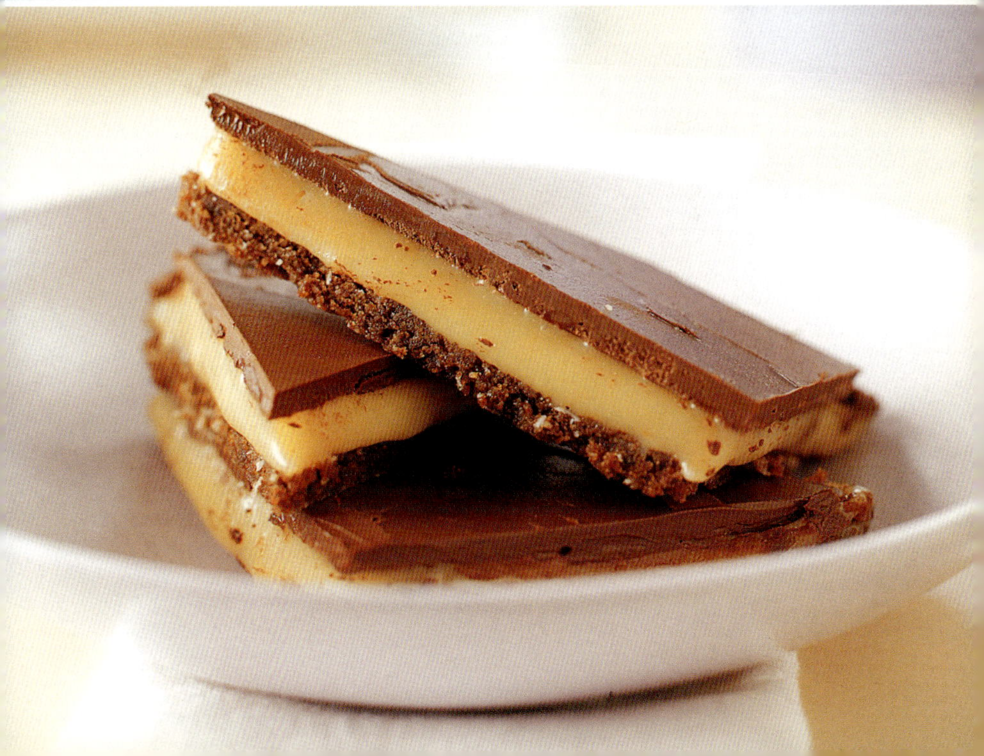

SESAME AND GINGER SLICE

Prep time: 15 minutes
Cooking time: 20 minutes
Makes 15 pieces

1 cup (125 g) plain flour
1/2 teaspoon bicarbonate
    of soda
1 teaspoon ground ginger
1/4 teaspoon mixed spice
2 eggs
3/4 cups (140 g) soft brown
    sugar
125 g unsalted butter,
    melted
1/4 cup (55 g) chopped
    crystallised ginger
1/3 cup (50 g) sesame
    seeds, toasted

1 Preheat the oven to moderate 180°C (350°F/ Gas 4). Lightly grease a 20 x 30 cm shallow baking tin and line with baking paper, leaving it hanging over the two long sides.
2 Sift together the flour, bicarbonate of soda, ginger, mixed spice and 1/4 teaspoon salt. Beat the eggs and brown sugar in a large bowl for 2 minutes, or until thick and creamy. Mix in the melted butter and gently fold in the flour mixture. Add the crystallised ginger and half the sesame seeds and mix gently.

Sesame and ginger slice
(top), and Bakewell slice

3 Spread into the tin and sprinkle evenly with the remaining sesame seeds. Bake for 20 minutes, or until firm to touch and slightly coloured. Cool in the tin for 10 minutes, then cool on a wire rack.

Nutrition per piece: Fat 9.5 g; Protein 3 g; Carbohydrate 19 g; Dietary Fibre 0.5 g; Cholesterol 45 mg; 695 kJ (165 cal)

BAKEWELL SLICE

Prep time: 30 minutes +
    30 minutes refrigeration
Cooking time: 45 minutes
Makes 15 pieces

1 cup (125 g) plain flour
1/4 cup (30 g) icing sugar
170 g unsalted butter,
    chilled and chopped
1 egg yolk
1/2 cup (125 g) caster sugar
4 eggs
2/3 cup (125 g) ground
    almonds
2 drops almond essence
1/2 cup (160 g) raspberry
    jam
1/4 cup (25 g) flaked
    almonds

1 Preheat the oven to moderate 180°C (350°F/ Gas 4). Lightly grease a 20 x 30 cm baking tin and line with baking paper, hanging over the two long sides.
2 Sift the flour and 1 tablespoon icing sugar

into a bowl, add 50 g butter and rub it in until the mixture resembles fine breadcrumbs. Add the egg yolk and 2 tablespoons cold water and mix with a flat-bladed knife until the mixture comes together in beads. Gather into a ball, cover with plastic wrap and refrigerate for 30 minutes. Roll out between two sheets of baking paper, remove the paper and place in the tin, pressing well into the edges. Bake for 10 minutes. Cool.
3 Beat the remaining butter and the caster sugar with electric beaters until creamy. Add the eggs and fold in the ground almonds and almond essence.
4 Spread the jam over the pastry base and pour the filling over the jam. Sprinkle with the flaked almonds and bake for 30–35 minutes, or until firm. Allow to cool.
5 Sift the remaining icing sugar into a bowl and mix in 2–3 teaspoons warm water to a free-flowing paste. Drizzle over the slice in a zigzag pattern and leave to set. Trim the edges and cut into squares.

Nutrition per piece: Fat 16.5 g; Protein 5 g; Carbohydrate 24 g; Dietary Fibre 1.5 g; Cholesterol 88.5 mg; 1095 kJ (269 cal)

PASSIONFRUIT AND COCONUT CHEESE SLICE

Prep time: 20 minutes +
  30 minutes refrigeration
Cooking time: 50 minutes
Makes 24 pieces

100 g slivered almonds
1 cup (125 g) plain flour
1 teaspoon baking powder
100 g unsalted butter,
  chopped
1/2 cup (125 g) caster sugar
1 egg yolk
1/4 cup (25 g) desiccated
  coconut
750 g cream cheese,
  softened
2 eggs
3/4 cup (185 ml) coconut
  milk
3 teaspoons vanilla essence
1/2 teaspoon lemon juice
3/4 cup (185 g) caster sugar,
  extra
65 g flaked almonds,
  toasted

Topping
3/4 cup (90 g) icing sugar
40 g unsalted butter,
  softened
1 tablespoon cornflour
2 tablespoons strained
  passionfruit juice

1 Finely chop the almonds in a food processor. Sift the flour and baking powder into a large mixing bowl. Add the butter and rub into the flour with your fingertips until it resembles breadcrumbs. Stir in the almonds and caster sugar. Make a well in the centre and add the egg yolk. Mix with a flat-bladed knife, using a cutting action, until the mixture comes together in beads. Add 2 tablespoons cold water if needed. Gently gather the mixture together and place on a lightly floured work surface. Shape into a ball, flatten slightly, wrap in plastic wrap and refrigerate for 30 minutes.
2 Preheat the oven to warm 170°C (325°F/ Gas 3). Lightly grease a 30 x 20 x 5 cm tin and line with baking paper, hanging over the two long sides. Roll the dough out to fit the base of the tin and press in evenly. Sprinkle the coconut over the base and lightly press it in. Bake for 10 minutes and cool for 10 minutes.
3 Combine the cream cheese and eggs in the food processor. Add the coconut milk, vanilla, lemon juice and extra sugar, and blend until smooth. Pour over the base and bake for 40 minutes, or until firm. Cool in the tin.
4 To make the topping, mix the icing sugar and butter with a wooden spoon until smooth. Stir in the cornflour, then gradually add the passionfruit juice. Mix until smooth, then spread over the slice. Scatter the flaked almonds over the top. Leave to set, remove from the tin and trim the edges, then cut into 5 cm squares.

Nutrition per piece: Fat 22 g; Protein 6 g; Carbohydrate 23 g; Dietary Fibre 1 g; Cholesterol 67.5 mg; 1270 kJ (305 cal)

Note: To toast the flaked almonds, spread the nuts on a baking tray and bake in a moderate 180°C (350°F/Gas 4) oven for 5–10 minutes, or until lightly golden. Keep a close eye on them, as they will brown quickly.

Passionfruit and coconut
cheese slice

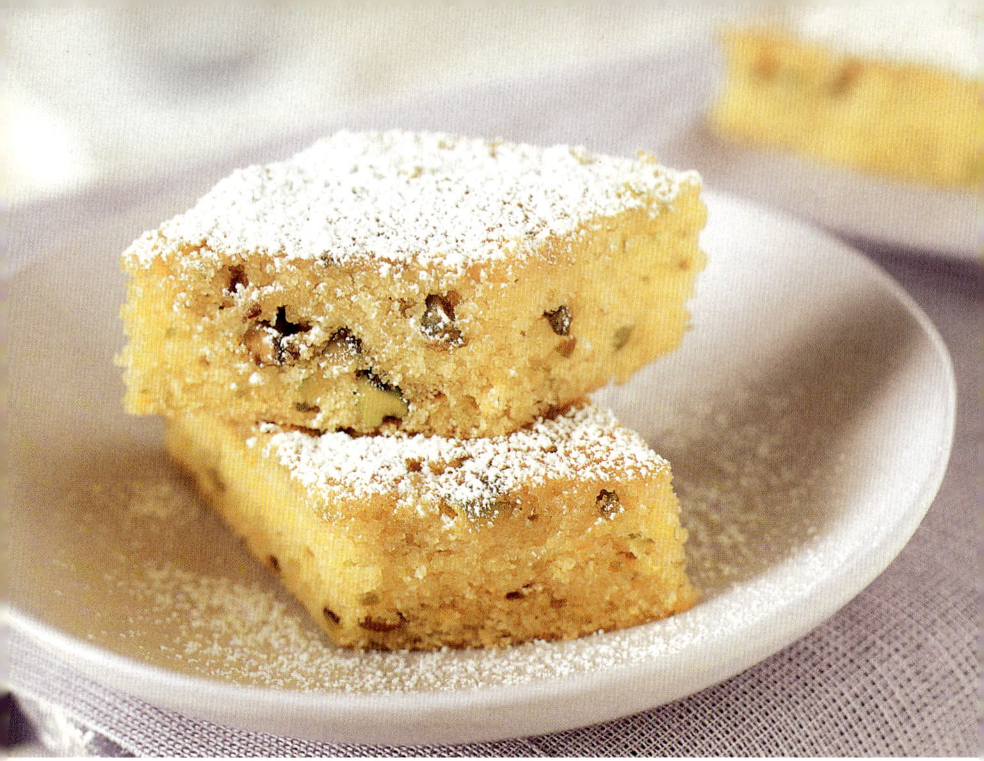

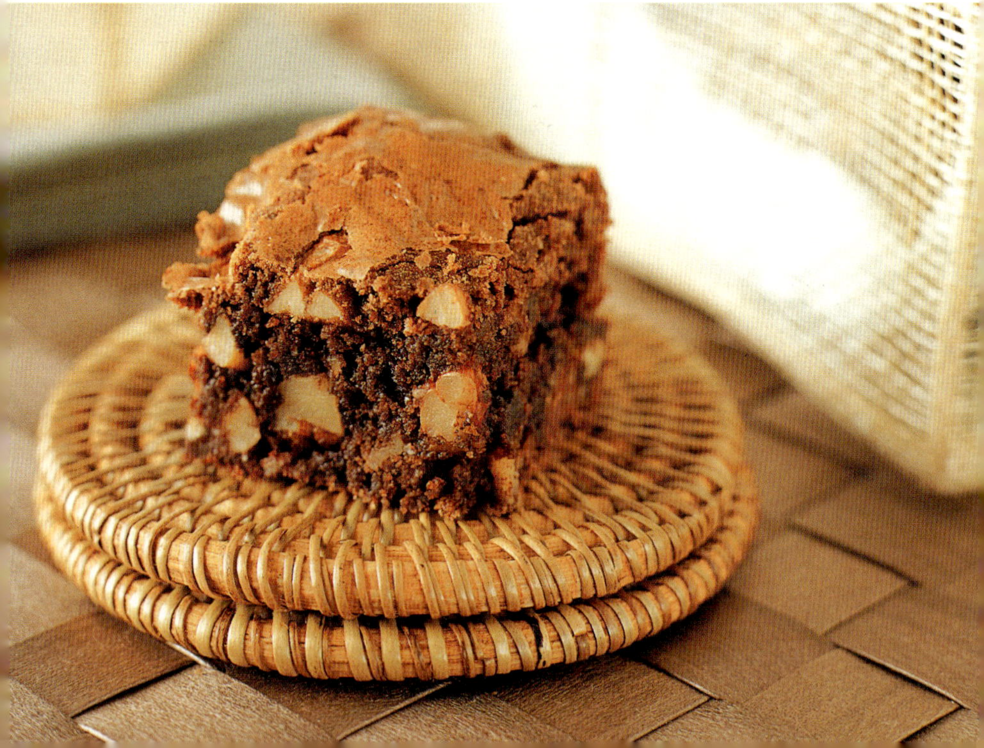

ORANGE, PISTACHIO AND SEMOLINA SLICE

Prep time: 20 minutes
Cooking time: 40 minutes
Makes 18 pieces

2/3 cup (100 g) shelled pistachios
200 g unsalted butter, chopped
2/3 cup (160 g) caster sugar
1 teaspoon vanilla essence
1 tablespoon finely grated orange rind
2 eggs
1/2 cup (60 g) self-raising flour, sifted
1/2 cup (125 ml) orange juice
1 1/2 cups (185 g) fine semolina
1 cup (250 g) caster sugar, extra
1/2 cup (125 ml) orange juice, extra
icing sugar, for dusting

1 Preheat the oven to moderate 180°C (350°F/ Gas 4). Lightly grease a 20 x 30 cm shallow baking tin and line with baking paper, leaving it hanging over on the two long sides.
2 Bake the pistachios for 8-10 minutes, or until lightly toasted. Cool, then chop.
3 Beat the butter and sugar with electric beaters until light and fluffy. Add the vanilla, rind and eggs and beat until combined.
4 Add the flour, juice, semolina and nuts, and fold in with a spatula until just combined—do not overmix. Spread into the tin. Bake for 30 minutes, or until golden brown and firm when lightly touched. Cool for 10 minutes in the tin, then on a wire rack placed on a tray.
5 Mix the extra sugar and orange juice in a small saucepan. Bring to the boil over medium heat, then simmer for 1 minute. Spoon over the slice. Cool and cut into squares or diamonds. Dust with icing sugar.

Nutrition per piece: Fat 13 g; Protein 4 g; Carbohydrate 34 g; Dietary Fibre 1 g; Cholesterol 48 mg; 1075 kJ (255 cal)

PECAN BROWNIES

Prep time: 15 minutes
Cooking time: 35 minutes
Makes 16 pieces

125 g dark chocolate
90 g unsalted butter, softened
1 cup (250 g) caster sugar
1 teaspoon vanilla essence
2 eggs
2/3 cup (80 g) plain flour
1/4 cup (30 g) cocoa powder
1/2 teaspoon baking powder
1 cup (125 g) roughly chopped pecans

1 Preheat the oven to moderate 180°C (350°F/ Gas 4). Grease a 17 cm square tin and line the base with baking paper hanging over two opposite sides.
2 Chop the chocolate into small even-sized pieces and place in a heatproof bowl. Bring a saucepan of water to the boil and remove from the heat. Sit the bowl over the pan—ensure the bowl doesn't touch the water. Stand, stirring occasionally, until melted. Cool slightly.
3 Beat the butter, sugar and vanilla with electric beaters until thick and creamy. Beat in the eggs one at a time, beating well after each addition. Stir in the chocolate.
4 Fold in the sifted combined flour, cocoa and baking powder with a metal spoon, then fold in the pecans. Spoon into the tin and smooth the surface. Bake for 30–35 minutes, or until firm and it comes away from the sides of the tin. Cool in the tin, remove and cut into squares.

Nutrition per piece: Fat 13.5 g; Protein 3 g; Carbohydrate 25 g; Dietary Fibre 1 g; Cholesterol 36.5 mg; 955 kJ (230 cal)

Orange, pistachio and semolina slice (top), and Pecan brownies

CINNAMON AND CHERRY SLICE

Prep time 20 minutes
Cooking time: 50 minutes
Makes 18 pieces

2 cups (250 g) self-raising flour
1 heaped teaspoon ground cinnamon
2 cups (370 g) soft brown sugar
125 g unsalted butter, chilled
720 g jar pitted morello cherries, drained
1 teaspoon baking powder
1 egg
300 ml cream
1 tablespoon lemon juice

1 Preheat the oven to moderate 180°C (350°F/Gas 4). Lightly grease a 20 x 30 cm shallow baking tin and line with baking paper, leaving the paper hanging over the two long sides.
2 Sift the flour and cinnamon into a bowl and stir in the sugar—transfer half to another bowl. Working quickly, grate the butter using a grater with large holes and divide between the bowls. Press half the mixture into the tin and bake for 10 minutes. Spread the cherries evenly over the base.
3 Add the baking powder to the reserved mixture and mix well. Lightly whisk the egg, cream and lemon juice in a bowl and add the reserved mixture, stirring well with a large metal spoon until combined. Spread over the cherries and bake for 40 minutes, or until a skewer comes out clean when inserted in the centre. Set aside to cool.

Nutrition per serve: Fat 13.5 g; Protein 3 g; Carbohydrate 32 g; Dietary Fibre 1 g; Cholesterol 50 mg; 1050 kJ (250 cal)

PECAN BLONDIES

Prep time: 20 minutes
Cooking time: 30 minutes
Makes 16 pieces

11/2 cups (185 g) plain flour
1 teaspoon baking powder
1 cup (250 g) caster sugar
1/2 cup (95 g) soft brown sugar
125 g unsalted butter, softened
1 teaspoon vanilla essence
2 eggs
1/2 cup (65 g) chopped pecans

Icing
150 g white chocolate, chopped
1/4 cup (60 ml) cream
2 tablespoons chopped pecans, extra

1 Preheat the oven to moderate 180°C (350°F/Gas 4). Lightly grease a 18 x 27 cm shallow baking tin and line the base and sides with baking paper, leaving the paper hanging over the two long sides.
2 Sift together the flour, baking powder and 1/4 teaspoon salt. Cream the sugars, butter and vanilla in a bowl and with electric beaters until light and fluffy. Gradually add the eggs, beating well after each addition. Fold in the flour with a large metal spoon and gently stir in the pecans. Spread the mixture into the tin.
3 Bake for 30 minutes, or until golden and a skewer inserted in the centre comes out clean. Leave in the tin for 10 minutes, then cool on a wire rack.
4 To make the icing, place the chocolate and cream in a small saucepan. Stir over low heat until the chocolate has melted and the mixture is smooth. Remove from the heat and cool. Spread evenly over the slice with a flat-bladed knife and sprinkle with the extra pecans. Allow to set.

Nutrition per piece: Fat 16 g; Protein 4 g; Carbohydrate 36 g; Dietary Fibre 1 g; Cholesterol 49 mg; 1235 kJ (295 cal)

Cinnamon and cherry slice (top), and Pecan blondies

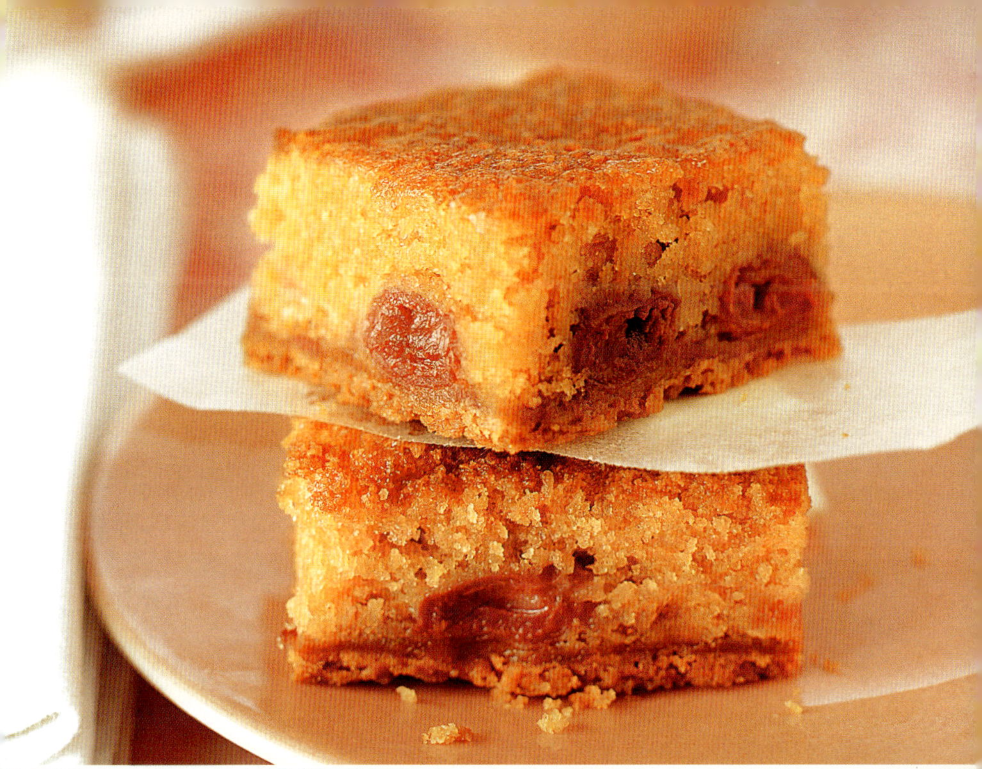

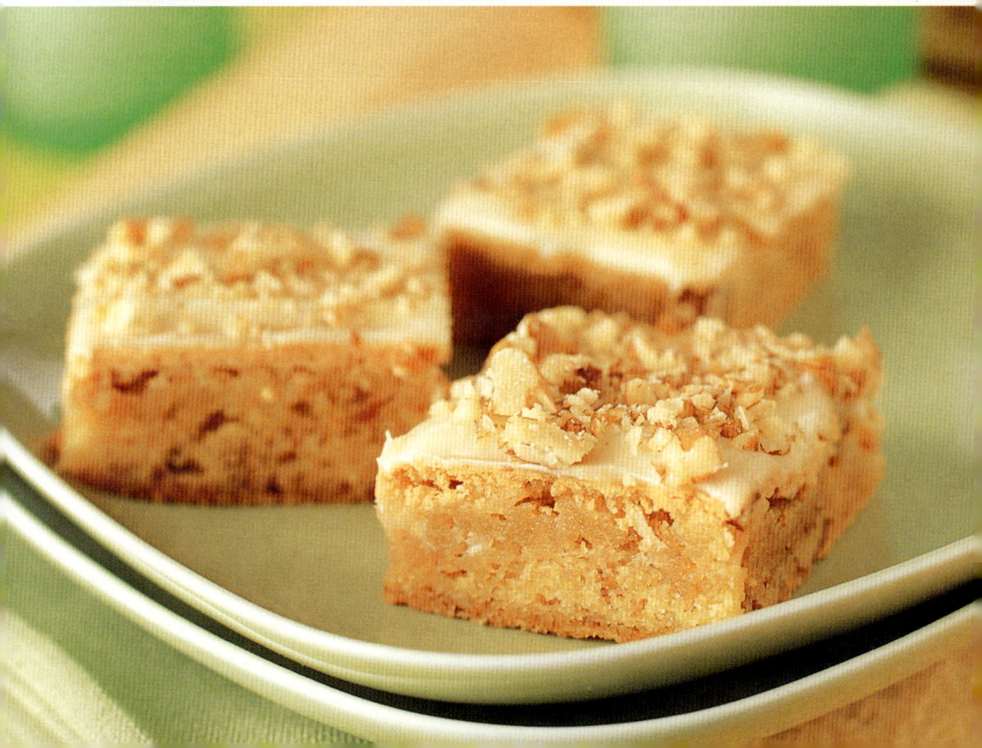

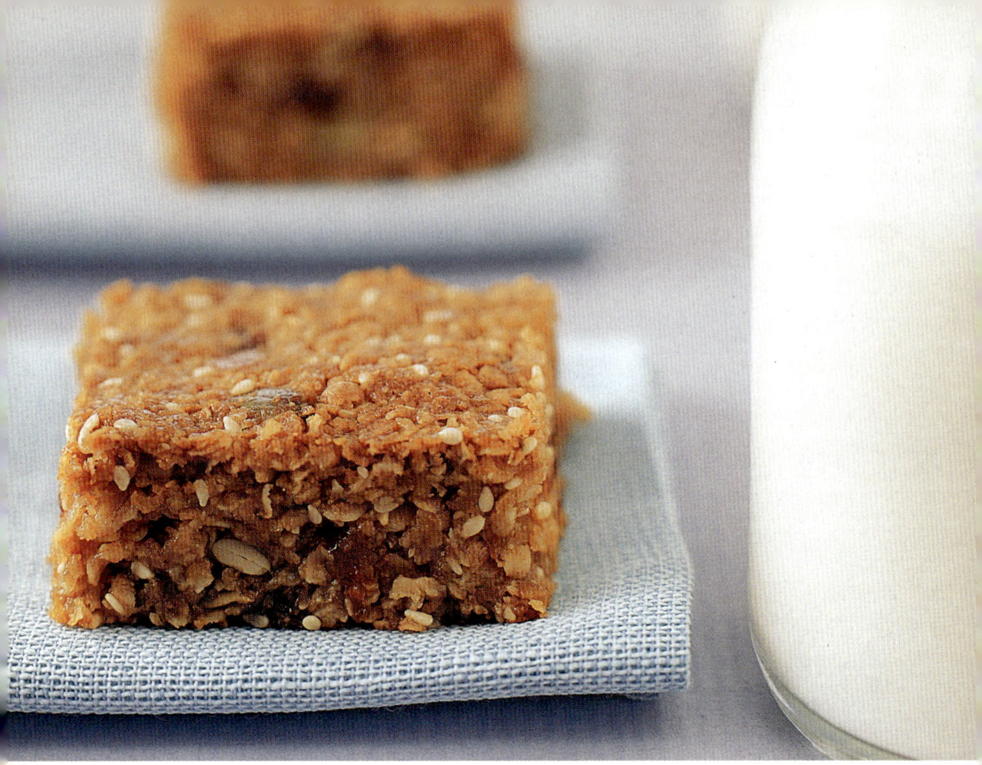

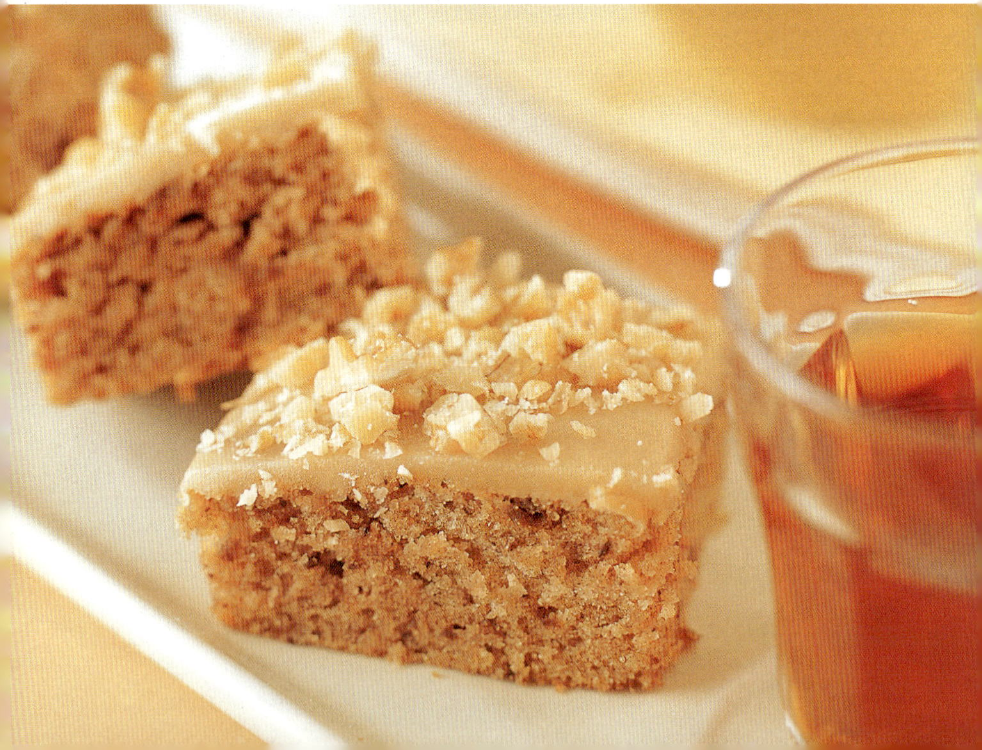

CHEWY FRUIT AND SEED SLICE

Prep time: 20 minutes
Cooking time: 25 minutes
Makes 18 pieces

200 g unsalted butter
1/2 cup (175 g) golden syrup
1/2 cup (125 g) crunchy peanut butter
2 teaspoons vanilla essence
1/4 cup (30 g) plain flour
1/3 cup (30 g) ground almonds
1/2 teaspoon mixed spice
3 cups (300 g) quick-cooking oats
2 teaspoons finely grated orange rind
1 cup (185 g) soft brown sugar
1/2 cup (45 g) desiccated coconut
1/3 cup (50 g) sesame seeds, toasted
1/2 cup (90 g) pepitas or shelled sunflower seeds
1/2 cup (80 g) raisins, chopped
1/4 cup (45 g) mixed peel

1 Preheat the oven to warm 170°C (325°F/ Gas 3). Lightly grease a 20 x 30 cm shallow tin and line with baking paper, hanging over the two long sides.
2 Place the butter and golden syrup in a small saucepan over low heat, stirring occasionally until melted. Remove from the heat and stir in the peanut butter and vanilla until combined.
3 Mix together the remaining ingredients, stirring well. Make a well in the centre and add the butter and syrup mixture. Mix with a large metal spoon until combined. Press evenly into the tin and bake for 25 minutes, or until golden and firm. Cool in the tin, then cut into squares.

Nutrition per piece: Fat 21 g; Protein 6 g; Carbohydrate 35 g; Dietary Fibre 3.5 g; Cholesterol 28 mg; 1445 kJ (345 cal)

STICKY TOFFEE SLICE

Prep time: 20 minutes
Cooking time: 35 minutes
Makes 18 pieces

250 g pitted dates, roughly chopped
1 teaspoon bicarbonate of soda
215 g unsalted butter
1 1/2 cups (185 g) self-raising flour
1 teaspoon vanilla essence
1 teaspoon baking powder
3 eggs
90 ml milk
2 tablespoons soft brown sugar
3/4 cup (90 g) icing sugar
3/4 cup (90 g) chopped walnuts

1 Preheat the oven to moderate 180°C (350°F/ Gas 4). Lightly grease a 20 x 30 cm baking tin and line with baking paper, hanging over the two long sides.
2 Place the dates in a saucepan with 200 ml water, bring to the boil, then reduce the heat and simmer gently for 10 minutes—make sure the water doesn't evaporate completely. Add the bicarbonate of soda and leave to cool.
3 Place 185 g of the butter, the flour, vanilla, baking powder, eggs and 75 ml of the milk in a food processor and mix in short bursts for 1 minute, or until well blended. Add the dates and pulse to blend. Do not overprocess.
4 Place the mixture in the tin and bake for 20 minutes, or until a skewer inserted in the centre comes out clean. Set aside to cool.
5 Place the remaining butter and milk and the brown sugar in a pan and heat gently to dissolve the sugar. Add the icing sugar and mix well. Spread over the cooled slice and sprinkle with the walnuts.

Nutrition per piece: Fat 14.5 g; Protein 4 g; Carbohydrate 24 g; Dietary Fibre 2 g; Cholesterol 61 mg; 980 kJ (235 cal)

Chewy fruit and seed slice (top), and Sticky toffee slice

PASSIONFRUIT AND LEMON DELICIOUS SLICE

Prep time: 15 minutes
Cooking time: 40 minutes
Makes 18 pieces

120 g unsalted butter, softened
1/2 cup (60 g) icing sugar, sifted
1/2 teaspoon vanilla essence
1 1/2 cups (185 g) plain flour, sifted
1 teaspoon grated lemon rind
icing sugar, for dusting

Filling
100 g plain flour
1/2 teaspoon baking powder
3/4 cup (65 g) desiccated coconut
3 eggs
1 cup (250 g) caster sugar
170 g can passionfriut pulp
2 tablespoons lemon juice
1 teaspoon grated lemon rind

1 Preheat the oven to moderate 180°C (350°F/Gas 4). Lightly grease a 18 x 27 cm baking tin and line with baking paper, leaving the paper hanging over the two long sides.
2 Cream the butter and icing sugar with electric beaters until pale and creamy, then add the vanilla. Fold in the flour and lemon rind with a large metal spoon. Press into the tin and bake for 15–20 minutes, or until lightly golden.
3 To make the filling, sift the flour and baking powder together and add the coconut. Lightly beat the eggs and sugar in a bowl, then add the passionfruit pulp, lemon juice and rind. Add the dry ingredients and stir until combined. Pour over the base and bake for 20 minutes, or until firm to touch. Cool in the tin. Dust with icing sugar and cut into pieces.

Nutrition per piece: Fat 9 g; Protein 4 g; Carbohydrate 31 g; Dietary Fibre 2.5 g; Cholesterol 47 mg; 895 kJ (215 cal)

GLACE FRUIT SLICE

Prep: 25 minutes
Cooking time: 25 minutes
Makes 24 pieces

2 cups (480 g) roughly chopped glacé fruit
2 tablespoons rum
100 g unsalted butter, softened
1/3 cup (90 g) caster sugar
2 eggs
2 teaspoons vanilla essence
1 cup (125 g) mixed toasted nuts, roughly chopped
1/4 cup (30 g) plain flour, sifted
1/4 cup (30 g) self-raising flour, sifted
1/4 cup (25 g) milk powder
2/3 cup (80 g) icing sugar
1 teaspoon rum, extra

1 Preheat the oven to moderately hot 190°C (375°F/Gas 5). Lightly grease an 18 x 27 cm shallow baking tin and line with baking paper, hanging over the two long sides.
2 Combine the glacé fruit and rum in a bowl. Beat the butter and sugar with electric beaters until light and fluffy. Add the eggs one at a time, beating well after each addition. Beat in the vanilla, then stir in the fruit mixture, nuts, flours and milk powder.
3 Spread evenly into the tin. Bake for 15 minutes, then reduce the oven to moderate 180°C (350°F/Gas 4) and bake for 10 minutes, or until golden brown. Cool in the tin until just warm.
4 Combine the icing sugar, extra rum and 1 teaspoon water until smooth and spreadable but not runny. If it's too thick, add a little more rum or water. Spread over the slice and cool completely. Cut into three lengthways strips, then cut each strip into eight pieces.

Nutrition per piece: Fat 7 g; Protein 3 g; Carbohydrate 24 g; Dietary Fibre 0.5 g; Cholesterol 26 mg; 685 kJ (165 cal)

Passionfruit and lemon delicious slice (top), and Glacé fruit slice

CHOCOLATE CASSATA SLICE

Prep time: 40 minutes + refrigeration
Cooking time: 30 minutes
Makes 16 pieces

125 g unsalted butter
125 g dark chocolate
1 cup (250 g) caster sugar
3 eggs, lightly beaten
1 teaspoon vanilla essence
1 cup (125 g) plain flour
1/4 cup (30 g) cocoa powder
1 cup (250 g) ricotta
1/3 cup (80 ml) thick cream
30 g caster sugar, extra
1/4 cup (60 ml) Grand Marnier or brandy
4 tablespoons coarsely chopped mixed candied fruit (cherries, peel, figs and cedro)
80 g semi-sweet chocolate, coarsely chopped
1/3 cup (50 g) roasted whole almonds, roughly chopped
50 ml Grand Marnier, extra
icing sugar, for dusting

1 Preheat the oven to moderate 180°C (350°F/ Gas 4). Lightly grease a 17 cm square shallow tin and line with baking paper, leaving the paper hanging over two opposite sides.
2 Chop the butter and dark chocolate into small even-sized pieces and put them in a heatproof bowl. Bring a saucepan of water to the boil and remove from the heat. Sit the bowl over the pan, making sure the bowl does not touch the water. Allow to stand, stirring occasionally, until the butter and chocolate have melted. Leave to cool slightly, then whisk in the extra caster sugar, eggs and vanilla essence.
3 Sift the flour and cocoa together, and stir gently into the chocolate mixture. Pour into the tin, smooth the surface and bake for 30 minutes, or until firm to touch. Remove from the oven and leave to cool.
4 Place the ricotta, cream, extra caster sugar, Grand Marnier, candied fruit, semi-sweet chocolate and almonds in a bowl and mix until well combined and smooth. Cover with plastic wrap and refrigerate until needed.
5 When the cake is completely cool, use a serrated knife to cut it in half horizontally. Brush the cut sides with the extra Grand Marnier. Line the cake tin with foil, leaving it hanging over all sides and place the bottom layer of the cake in the tin, cut-side-up. Spread carefully with the ricotta mixture and smooth the surface. Place the remaining cake layer over the top and press firmly. Trim with a serrated knife and cut into squares. Dust with icing sugar to serve.

Nutrition per piece: Fat 17 g; Protein 6 g; Carbohydrate 35 g; Dietary Fibre 1 g; Cholesterol 66.5 mg; 1335 kJ (320 cal)

Note: There are two types of dessert dishes called 'cassata'. One is an ice cream dessert, and the other is a traditional Sicilian cake made with ricotta and candied fruit—this slice is a variation on the Sicilian dish.

Chocolate cassata slice

CIDER CRUMBLE SLICE

Prep time: 20 minutes
Cooking time: 35 minutes
Makes 24 pieces

60 g unsalted butter
1 1/2 tablespoons golden syrup
150 ml alcoholic apple cider
2 cups (250 g) self-raising flour
1/8 teaspoon ground ginger
1/4 cup (50 g) soft brown sugar
70 g pitted dates, chopped
150 g walnuts, chopped
1 egg
1 large Granny Smith apple
2 1/2 tablespoons caster sugar
1/2 cup (60 g) plain flour

1 Preheat the oven to warm 170°C (325°F/ Gas 3). Lightly grease a 20 x 30 cm baking tin and line with baking paper, hanging over on the two long sides.
2 Melt 20 g butter and the golden syrup in a saucepan. Remove from the heat and stir in the cider. Sift the flour and ginger into a bowl. Stir in the brown sugar, dates and half the nuts. Beat in the golden syrup mixture and egg until smooth. Spoon into the tin.
3 Peel, core and thinly slice the apple, then cut into 1.5 cm pieces. Melt the remaining butter in a small saucepan, add the caster sugar, flour, apple and remaining nuts and stir well. Spread over the cake mixture. Bake for 30 minutes, or until golden and a skewer comes out clean. Cool in the tin, remove and cut into squares.

Nutrition per piece: Fat 7 g; Protein 3 g; Carbohydrate 18 g; Dietary Fibre 1.5 g; Cholesterol 14 mg; 590 kJ (140 cal)

APRICOT AND MACAROON SLICE

Prep time: 20 minutes +
  30 minutes soaking
Cooking time: 50 minutes
Makes 16 pieces

100 g unsalted butter, softened
1/3 cup (90 g) caster sugar
1 egg
1 1/3 cups (185 g) plain flour
1/2 teaspoon baking powder

Filling
250 g dried apricots, roughly chopped
1 tablespoon Grand Marnier
2 tablespoons caster sugar

Topping
100 g unsalted butter
1/3 cup (90 g) caster sugar
1 teaspoon vanilla essence
2 eggs
3 cups (270 g) desiccated coconut
1/3 cup (40 g) plain flour
1/2 teaspoon baking powder

1 Preheat the oven to moderate 180°C (350°F/ Gas 4). Lightly grease a 20 x 30 cm baking tin and line with baking paper. Cream the butter and sugar until light and fluffy. Add the egg and beat well. Sift the flour and baking powder and fold into the butter mixture with a metal spoon. Press firmly into the tin and bake for 20-25 minutes, or until golden brown. Cool.
2 To make the filling, combine the apricots, Grand Marnier, sugar and 1/2 cup (125 ml) boiling water in a bowl. Set aside for 30 minutes, then purée in a food processor. Spread evenly over the cooled base.
3 To make the topping, cream the butter, sugar and vanilla until light and fluffy. Gradually add the eggs, beating well after each addition. Fold in the coconut, flour and baking powder with a large metal spoon. Spoon onto the apricot leaving it lumpy and loose—do not press down. Bake for 20-25 minutes, or until lightly golden.

Nutrition per piece: Fat 22.5 g; Protein 5 g; Carbohydrate 32 g; Dietary Fibre 4.5 g; Cholesterol 65.5 mg; 1440 kJ (345 cal)

Cider crumble slice (top), and Apricot and macaroon slice

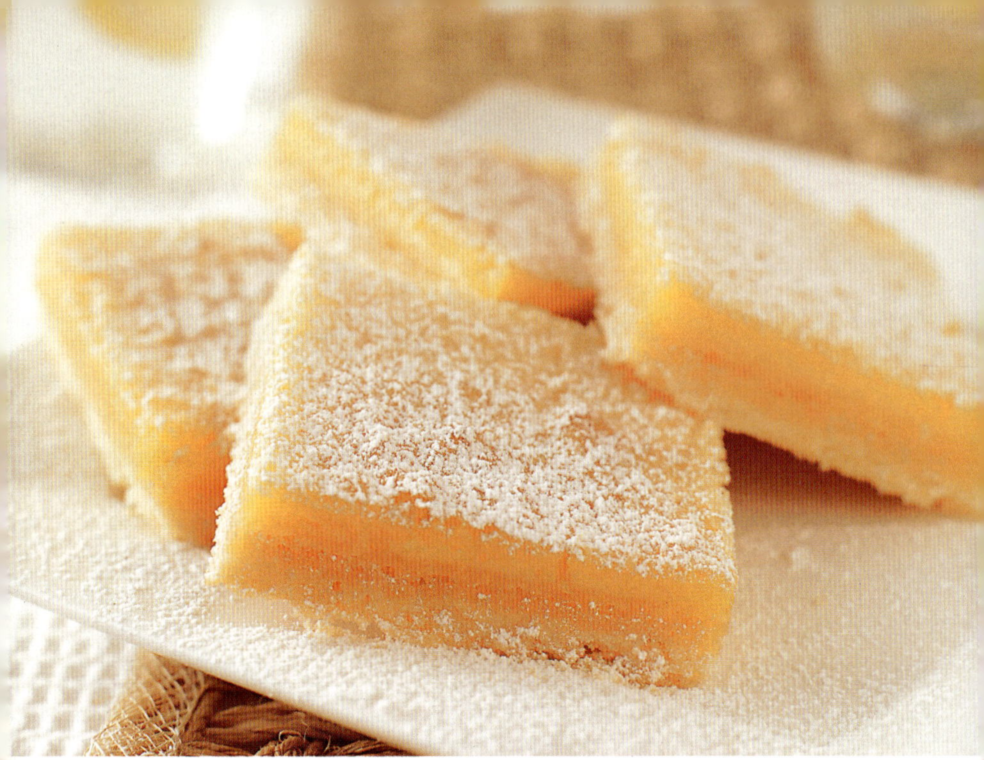

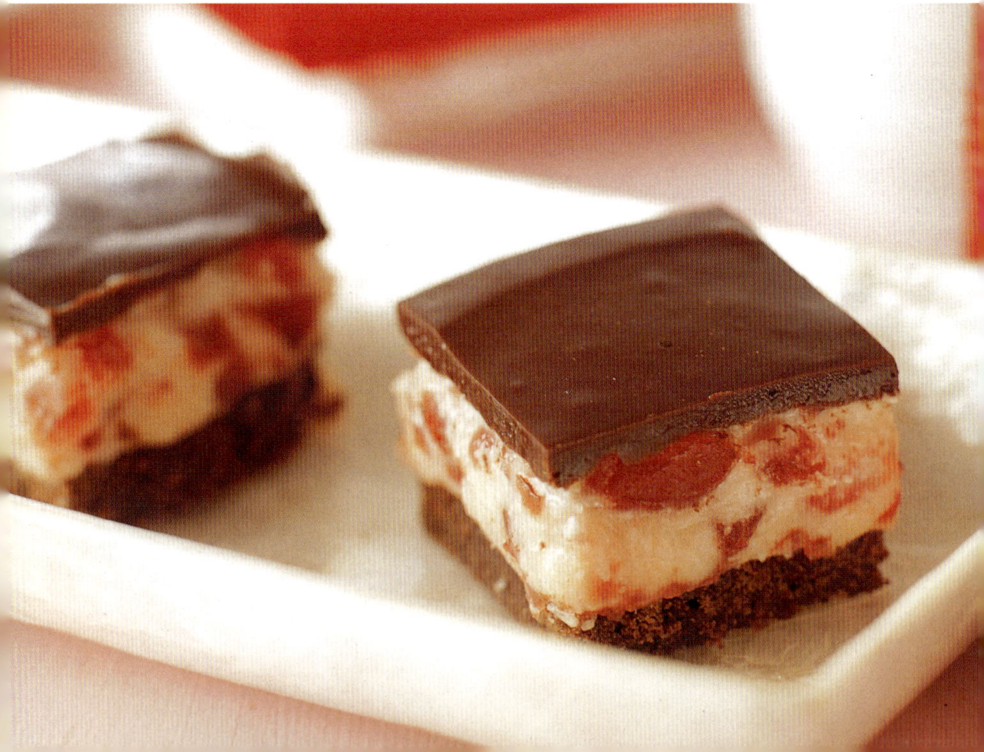

LEMON SQUARES

Prep time: 20 minutes
Cooking time: 45 minutes
Makes 30 pieces

125 g unsalted butter
75g caster sugar
11/4 cups (155 g) plain flour,
  sifted
icing sugar, for dusting

Topping
4 eggs, lightly beaten
1 cup (250 g) caster sugar
1/2 cup (60 ml) lemon juice
1 teaspoon finely grated
  lemon rind
1/4 cup (30 g) plain flour
1/2 teaspoon baking powder

1 Preheat the oven to
moderate 180°C (350°F/
Gas 4). Lightly grease
a 20 x 30 cm slice tin
and line with baking
paper, leaving the
paper hanging over
two opposite sides.
2 Cream the butter
and sugar with electric
beaters until pale and
fluffy. Fold in the flour
with a metal spoon. Press
into the tin and bake
for 20 minutes, or until
golden and firm. Cool.
3 Beat the eggs and
sugar with electric
beaters for 2 minutes, or
until light and fluffy. Stir
in the lemon juice and
rind. Sift together the
flour and baking powder

Lemon squares (top), and
Glacé cherry slice

and gradually whisk into
the egg mixture. Pour
onto the base. Bake for
25 minutes, or until just
firm. Cool in the tin and
dust with icing sugar.

Nutrition per piece: Fat 4 g;
Protein 2 g; Carbohydrate 16 g;
Dietary Fibre 0.5 g; Cholesterol
34.5 mg; 435 kJ (105 cal)

GLACE
CHERRY SLICE

Prep time: 20 minutes +
  50 minutes refrigeration
Cooking time: 20 minutes
Makes 28 pieces

1 cup (125 g) plain flour
1/3 cup (40 g) cocoa powder
1/3 cup (90 g) caster sugar
125 g unsalted butter,
  melted
1 teaspoon vanilla essence
2 cups (420 g) glacé
  cherries, finely chopped
1/2 cup (60 g) icing sugar
11/2 cups (135 g)
  desiccated coconut
1/2 cup (160 g) condensed
  milk
60 g unsalted butter, melted
50 g white vegetable
  shortening (Copha), melted
150 g dark cooking
  chocolate
25 g unsalted butter, extra
2 tablespoons cream

1 Preheat the oven to
moderate 180°C (350°F/
Gas 4). Lightly grease
a 18 x 27 cm shallow
baking tin and line with

baking paper, leaving
the paper hanging over
the two long sides.
2 Sift the flour, cocoa
and sugar into a bowl,
add the butter and
vanilla, and mix to form
a dough. Gather together
and turn onto a well-
floured surface. Press
together for 1 minute,
then press into the base
of the tin. Chill for
20 minutes. Cover
with baking paper
and baking beads or
uncooked rice and
bake for 10–15 minutes.
Remove the paper and
beads and bake for
5 minutes. Cool.
3 Combine the cherries,
icing sugar and coconut.
Stir in the condensed
milk, butter and Copha,
then spread over the
cooled base. Chill for
30 minutes.
4 Chop the chocolate
and extra butter into
small even-sized pieces
and place in a heatproof
bowl. Bring a saucepan
of water to the boil and
remove from the heat.
Sit the bowl over the
pan, making sure the
bowl doesn't touch the
water. Allow to stand,
stirring occasionally until
melted. Pour over the
cooled cherry mixture,
then chill until set.

Nutrition per piece: Fat 14 g;
Protein 2 g; Carbohydrate 26 g;
Dietary Fibre 1 g; Cholesterol
23 mg; 975 kJ (235 cal)

CHOCOLATE PEANUT SQUARES

Prep time: 20 minutes
Cooking time: 30 minutes
Makes 24 pieces

200 g dark chocolate
125 g unsalted butter
1 cup (230 g) firmly packed
   soft brown sugar
3/4 cup (65 g) crunchy
   peanut butter
2 eggs
1 cup (125 g) plain flour
1/4 cup (30 g) self-raising
   flour
1/2 cup (80 g) unsalted
   roasted peanuts, roughly
   chopped
100 g dark chocolate, extra,
   broken into pieces

1 Preheat the oven to warm 170°C (325°F/ Gas 3). Lightly grease an 18 x 27 cm baking tin and line with baking paper, hanging over the two long sides.
2 Chop the chocolate into small even-sized pieces and place in a heatproof bowl. Bring a saucepan of water to the boil and remove from the heat. Sit the bowl over the pan—ensure the bowl doesn't touch the water. Allow to stand, stirring occasionally, until melted. Cool.
3 Cream the butter, sugar and peanut butter with electric beaters until thick. Add the eggs one at a time, beating well after each addition. Stir in the chocolate, sifted flours and peanuts.
4 Spread the mixture into the tin and gently press the pieces of dark chocolate evenly into the surface. Bake for 30 minutes, or until a skewer inserted into the centre comes out clean. Cool in the tin.

Nutrition per piece: Fat 11.5 g; Protein 4 g; Carbohydrate 23 g; Dietary Fibre 1 g; Cholesterol 28 mg; 840 kJ (200 cal)

GINGER CHEESECAKE SLICE

Prep time: 20 minutes +
   30 minutes refrigeration
Cooking time: 25 minutes
Makes 24 pieces

200 g ginger-flavoured
   biscuits, finely crushed
60 g unsalted butter, melted
1/2 teaspoon ground
   cinnamon
500 g cream cheese
1/2 cup (125 ml) golden
   syrup
2 tablespoons caster sugar
2 eggs, lightly beaten
1/4 cup (55 g) finely
   chopped crystallised
   ginger
1/2 cup (125 ml) cream,
   lightly whipped
1/2 cup (125 ml) cream, extra
2 teaspoons caster sugar,
   extra
1/4 cup (55 g) crystallised
   ginger, extra, thinly sliced

1 Preheat the oven to warm 170°C (325°F/ Gas 3). Lightly grease a 20 x 30 cm baking tin and line with baking paper, leaving the paper hanging over the two long sides.
2 Combine the biscuits, butter and cinnamon, press into the base of the tin. Refrigerate for 30 minutes, or until firm.
3 Beat the cream cheese, golden syrup and sugar with electric beaters until light and fluffy. Add the eggs, one at a time, beating well after each addition. Fold in the ginger and whipped cream. Spread over the base and bake for 25 minutes, or until just set. Turn off the oven and cool with the door slightly ajar.
4 Remove from the tin and trim the edges. Beat the extra cream and extra sugar until soft peaks form and spread over the cheesecake. Using a hot dry knife, cut into three strips lengthways and then cut each strip into eight pieces. Decorate with the extra ginger.

Nutrition per piece: Fat 15 g; Protein 3 g; Carbohydrate 18 g; Dietary Fibre 0.5 g; Cholesterol 56.5 mg; 885 kJ (210 cal)

Chocolate peanut
squares (top), and
Ginger cheesecake slice

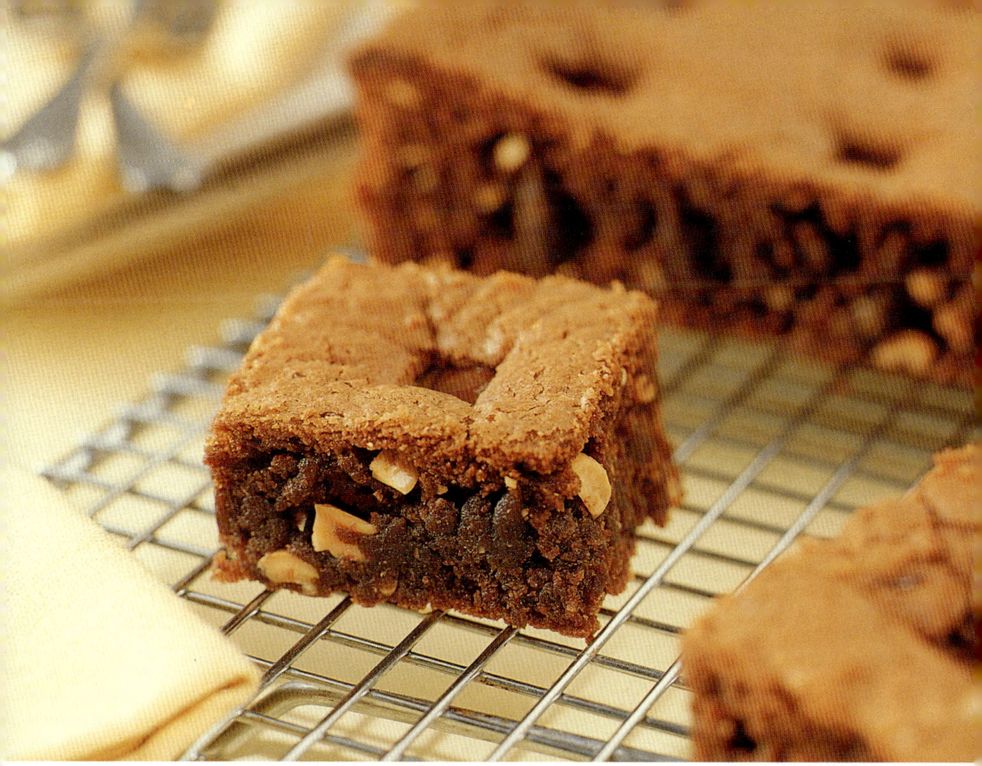

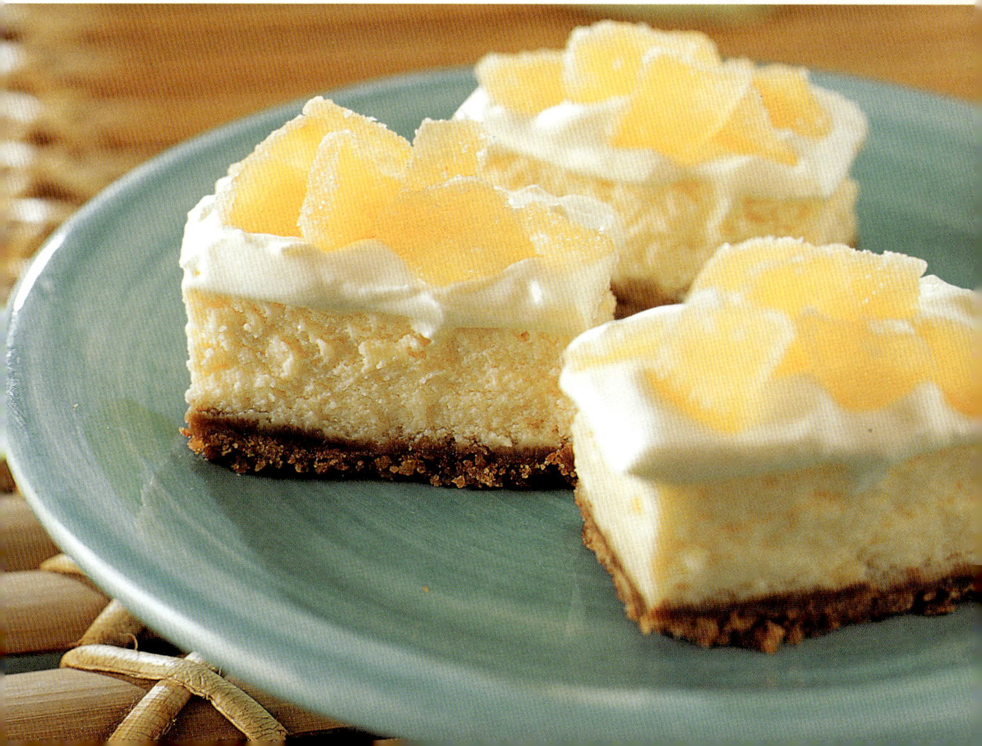

CURRANT SLICE

Prep time: 25 minutes +
30 minutes refrigeration +
20 minutes standing
Cooking time: 45 minutes
Makes 18 pieces

2 cups (250 g) self-raising
flour
1 tablespoon custard
powder
120 g unsalted butter,
chilled and chopped
1/2 cup (125 g) caster sugar
1 egg yolk

Filling
1 cup (150 g) currants
1 tablespoon Madeira
1 cup (185 g) soft brown
sugar
60 g unsalted butter,
softened
1 egg, lightly beaten
1/2 teaspoon vanilla
essence
1/4 teaspoon mixed spice
1 egg white, lightly beaten
1 1/2 tablespoons caster
sugar

1 Sift the flour and custard powder together into a large bowl. Rub the butter into the flour with your finger until the mixture resembles fine breadcrumbs, then stir in the sugar. Make a well in the centre and add the egg yolk and 2 tablespoons water and mix with a flat-bladed knife, using a cutting action, until the mixture comes together in beads. Add more water if necessary to bring the dough together. Gently gather the dough together and lift out onto a lightly floured work surface. Press together into a ball and flatten slightly into a disc. Wrap in plastic wrap and refrigerate for 30 minutes.

2 Preheat the oven to moderate 180°C (350°F/Gas 4). Lightly grease a 18 x 27 cm baking tin and line the base and sides with baking paper, leaving the paper hanging over the two long sides. This makes it easier to lift the cooked slice from the tin.

3 To make the filling, place the currants and Madeira in a large bowl and pour in 1/2 cup (125 ml) boiling water. Leave to stand for 20 minutes. Drain the currants well, squeeze out any excess liquid and return to the bowl. Add the sugar, butter, egg, vanilla essence and mixed spice and beat until the butter is smooth and fully blended in.

4 Divide the dough in half. Roll the first half out on a sheet of baking paper to a 19 x 29 cm rectangle. Transfer to the base of the baking tin, trimming the edges so that the dough runs up the sides 5 mm all around. Spread the filling over the top. Roll the second half of dough out to the same size as the first and place over the filling to cover. Neaten the edges with a knife then press them down onto the dough below, enclosing the filling. Don't worry if the top cracks because it will be covered.

5 Brush the surface with egg white and sprinkle the caster sugar over the top. Bake on the middle rack for 45 minutes. Cover with foil after 25 minutes to prevent the top from browning too much. Cool in the tin. Using a serrated knife, cut into slices. Keeps for 3-4 days in an airtight container.

Nutrition per piece: Fat 9 g; Protein 2.5 g; Carbohydrate 34 g; Dietary Fibre 1 g; Cholesterol 45 mg; 935 kJ (225 cal)

Currant slice

RUM AND RAISIN SLICE

Prep time: 25 minutes + overnight refrigeration
Cooking time: 35 minutes
Makes 20 pieces

1/4 cup (60 g) raisins
1/3 cup (80 ml) dark rum
200 g dark chocolate
60 g unsalted butter
1/2 cup (125 g) caster sugar
1 cup (250 ml) thick cream
1 cup (125 g) plain flour
3 eggs, lightly beaten
cocoa powder, for dusting

1 Preheat the oven to moderate 180°C (350°F/Gas 4). Lightly grease a 18 x 28 cm shallow baking tin and line with baking paper, hanging over on two opposite sides.
2 Combine the raisins and rum. Chop the chocolate and butter into small even-sized pieces and place in a heatproof bowl. Bring a saucepan of water to the boil and remove from the heat. Sit the bowl over the pan—ensure the bowl doesn't touch the water. Allow to stand, stirring occasionally, until melted. Stir in the caster sugar and cream.
3 Sift the flour into a bowl. Add the raisins, chocolate mixture and eggs and mix well. Pour into the tin and smooth the surface. Bake for 25-30 minutes, or until just set. Cool completely, then refrigerate overnight before cutting into small pieces. Sprinkle liberally with cocoa powder.

Nutrition per piece: Fat 10.5 g; Protein 3 g; Carbohydrate 20 g; Dietary Fibre 0.5 g; Cholesterol 49 mg; 795 kJ (190 cal)

CHOCOLATE CHEESE SWIRLS

Prep time: 20 minutes
Cooking time: 1 hour
Makes 24 pieces

1.25 kg cream cheese, at room temperature
120 g ricotta
3 teaspoons vanilla essence
1 1/4 cups (310 g) caster sugar
6 eggs
100 g dark chocolate, broken into squares
1 tablespoon rum
2 teaspoons powdered drinking chocolate
75 g ground hazelnuts
3 teaspoons grated orange rind
50 g crushed amaretti biscuits
icing sugar, for dusting

1 Preheat the oven to warm 170°C (325°F/Gas 3). Lightly grease a 20 x 30 cm tin and line with baking paper, hanging over the two long sides.
2 Blend the cream cheese, ricotta, vanilla and sugar in a food processor until smooth. Add the eggs and process until smooth. Divide the mixture between two bowls.
3 Bring a saucepan of water to the boil and remove from the heat. Put the chocolate, rum and drinking chocolate in a heatproof bowl and place over the water— ensure the bowl doesn't touch the water. Stir occasionally until melted. Cool and add to one bowl. Mix well, stir in the hazelnuts and pour into the tin.
4 Stir the orange rind and biscuits into the other bowl of cream cheese. Mix well, then gently spoon over the chocolate mix, covering completely. With a knife and starting in one corner, cut the orange mix down through the chocolate, bringing the chocolate up in swirls through the orange.
5 Bake for 1 hour, or until set. Cool in the tin. Turn out, trim away the edges and cut into 4 cm squares. Dust with icing sugar.

Nutrition per piece: Fat 22.5 g; Protein 8 g; Carbohydrate 19 g; Dietary Fibre 0.5 g; Cholesterol 98 mg; 1270 kJ (305 cal)

Rum and raisin slice (top), and Chocolate cheese swirls

CHESTNUT CREAM AND CHOCOLATE SLICE

Prep time: 50 minutes + refrigeration
Cooking time: 40 minutes
Makes 16 pieces

Sponge
1/3 cup (40 g) self-raising flour
1/4 cup (30 g) plain flour
1 tablespoon Dutch cocoa powder
1/4 cup (60 g) caster sugar
1 egg, lightly beaten
1 teaspoon vanilla essence
65 g unsalted butter, softened
1/4 cup (60 ml) milk
1/4 cup (60 ml) brandy

Base
1/2 cup (60 g) plain flour
2 tablespoons Dutch cocoa powder
2 tablespoons caster sugar
60 g unsalted butter, melted
1 tablespoon milk
1/2 teaspoon vanilla essence

Chestnut cream
30 g unsalted butter
1 cup (260 g) unsweetened chestnut purée
1/2 cup (60 g) icing sugar
2 tablespoons brandy

Chocolate glaze
60 g unsalted butter
100 g good-quality dark chocolate
1 tablespoon cream

Chestnut cream and chocolate slice

1 Preheat the oven to moderate 180°C (350°F/Gas 4). Grease a 17 cm square shallow tin and line with baking paper.
2 To make the sponge, sift the flours and the cocoa into a bowl, stir in the sugar and make a well in the centre. Combine the egg, vanilla, butter and milk and stir into the well until just combined. Spoon into the tin and bake for 10–15 minutes, or until it springs back when lightly touched. Cool completely. Using a serrated knife, cut in half on the horizontal. Brush the cut sides with brandy. Increase the oven to moderately hot 190°C (375°F/Gas 5).
3 To make the base, lightly grease a 17 cm square shallow tin and line with baking paper, leaving the paper hanging over two opposite sides. Sift the flour, cocoa and sugar into a bowl. Add the butter, milk and vanilla and mix well to form a dough. Gently gather together on a lightly floured surface for 1 minute, adding more flour if sticky. Press into the tin and refrigerate for 20 minutes.
4 Cover the pastry with baking paper, fill with baking beads or uncooked rice and bake for 10-15 minutes, or until dry. Remove the paper and beads. Reduce the oven to moderate 180°C (350°F/Gas 4). Bake for 8–10 minutes, or until firm. Leave to cool.
4 To make the chestnut cream, beat the butter, chestnut purée, icing sugar and brandy in a bowl until smooth. Spread half over the base and place one layer of chocolate sponge on top, pressing gently. Repeat with the remaining chestnut cream and sponge.
5 To make the glaze, chop the butter and chocolate into small even-sized pieces and put in a small heatproof bowl with the cream. Bring a small saucepan of water to the boil and remove from the heat. Sit the bowl over the pan, making sure the bowl doesn't touch the water. Allow to stand, stirring occasionally, until the chocolate and butter have melted. Remove the bowl from the pan and stir until well combined. Cool before spreading on the slice.

Nutrition per piece: Fat 14.5 g; Protein 3 g; Carbohydrate 24 g; Dietary Fibre 0.5 g; Cholesterol 47.5 mg; 1025 kJ (245 cal)

PEANUT TOFFEE SHORTBREAD

Prep time: 15 minutes +
10 minutes resting
Cooking time: 25 minutes
Makes 18 pieces

290 g unsalted butter
1/2 cup (125 g) caster sugar
1 egg
1 1/2 cups (185 g) plain flour, sifted
1/2 cup (60 g) self-raising flour, sifted
1 cup (180 g) soft brown sugar
2 tablespoons golden syrup
1/2 teaspoon lemon juice
400 g roasted unsalted peanuts

1 Preheat the oven to moderate 180°C (350°F/ Gas 4). Lightly grease a 18 x 27 cm baking tin and line the base and sides with baking paper hanging over the two long sides.
2 Cream 110 g butter and the caster sugar with electric beaters until light and fluffy. Add the egg and beat well. Fold in the sifted flours with a large metal spoon until just combined. Press into the tin and bake for 15 minutes, or until firm and lightly coloured. Cool for 10 minutes.
3 Place the soft brown sugar, golden syrup, juice and remaining butter in a saucepan. Stir over low heat until the sugar has dissolved. Simmer, stirring, for 5 minutes. Stir in the peanuts. Spread evenly over the base using two spoons—careful as the mixture is very hot. Bake for a further 5 minutes. Leave to cool in the tin for 15 minutes. Turn out and cut into fingers.

Nutrition per piece: Fat 24.5 g; Protein 8 g; Carbohydrate 31 g; Dietary Fibre 2.5 g; Cholesterol 50.5 mg; 1535 kJ (365 cal)

FLORENTINE SLICE

Prep time: 20 minutes
Cooking time: 1 hour
Makes 20 pieces

325 g unsalted butter
1/2 cup (125 g) caster sugar
1 1/2 cups (185 g) plain flour, sifted
1 teaspoon baking powder
2 tablespoons custard powder
1 egg yolk
2 cups (180 g) flaked almonds
200 g glacé cherries
100 g mixed peel
1 cup (145 g) craisins (sun-dried cranberries)
1 cup (350 g) honey
30 g dark chocolate, melted

1 Preheat the oven to moderate 180°C (350°F/ Gas 4). Lightly grease a 20 x 30 cm baking tin and line the base and sides with baking paper hanging over the two long sides.
2 Mix 125 g butter, the sugar, 1 1/4 cups (155 g) flour, the baking powder and custard powder in a food processor in short bursts for 1 minute, or until combined. Add 2 teaspoons water and the egg yolk and mix in short bursts until it resembles moist crumbs.
3 Place the mixture in the tin and flatten down well. Bake for 20 minutes, then leave to cool slightly.
4 Place the almonds, cherries, peel and craisins in a large bowl. Melt the honey and remaining butter, then whisk in the remaining flour. Add to the fruit and mix well. Pour over the base and bake for 40 minutes. Leave to cool. When cold, drizzle with the melted chocolate in a zigzag pattern. When set, cut into squares.

Nutrition per piece: Fat 19.5 g; Protein 4 g; Carbohydrate 49 g; Dietary Fibre 1.5 g; Cholesterol 50 mg; 1510 kJ (360 cal)

Peanut toffee shortbread (top), and Florentine slice

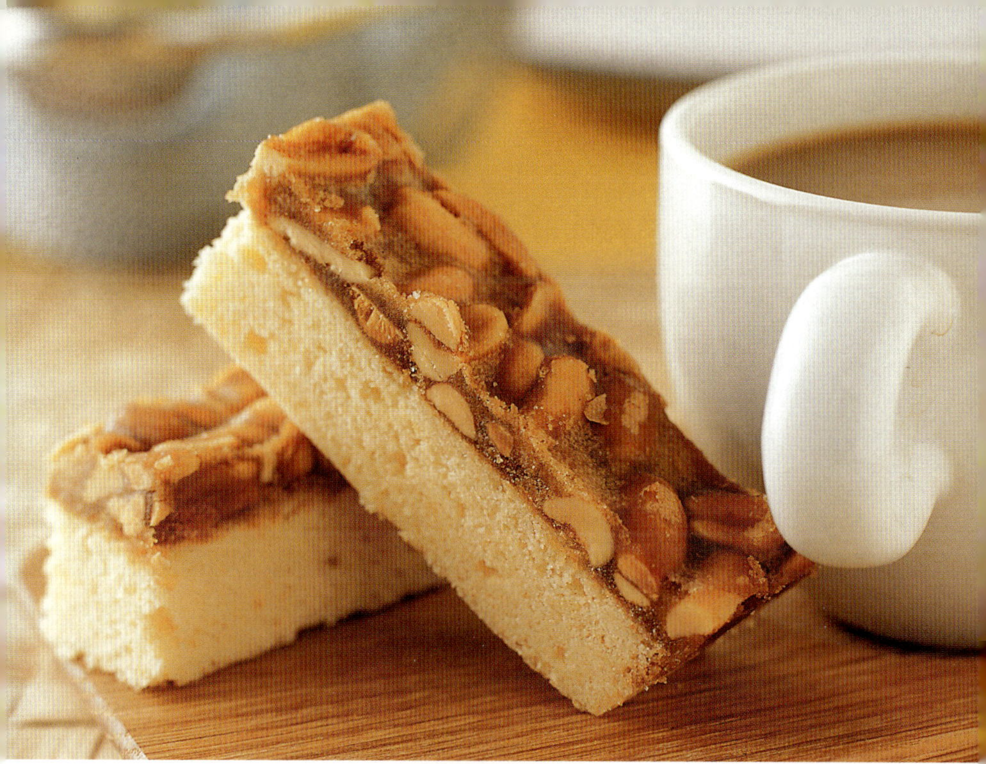

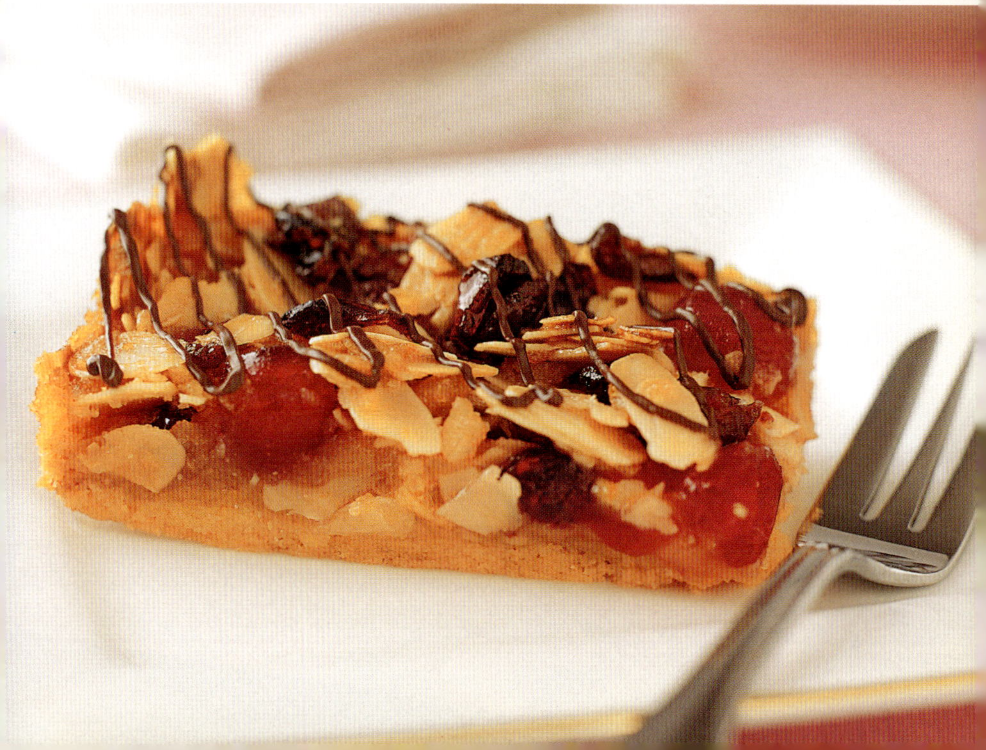

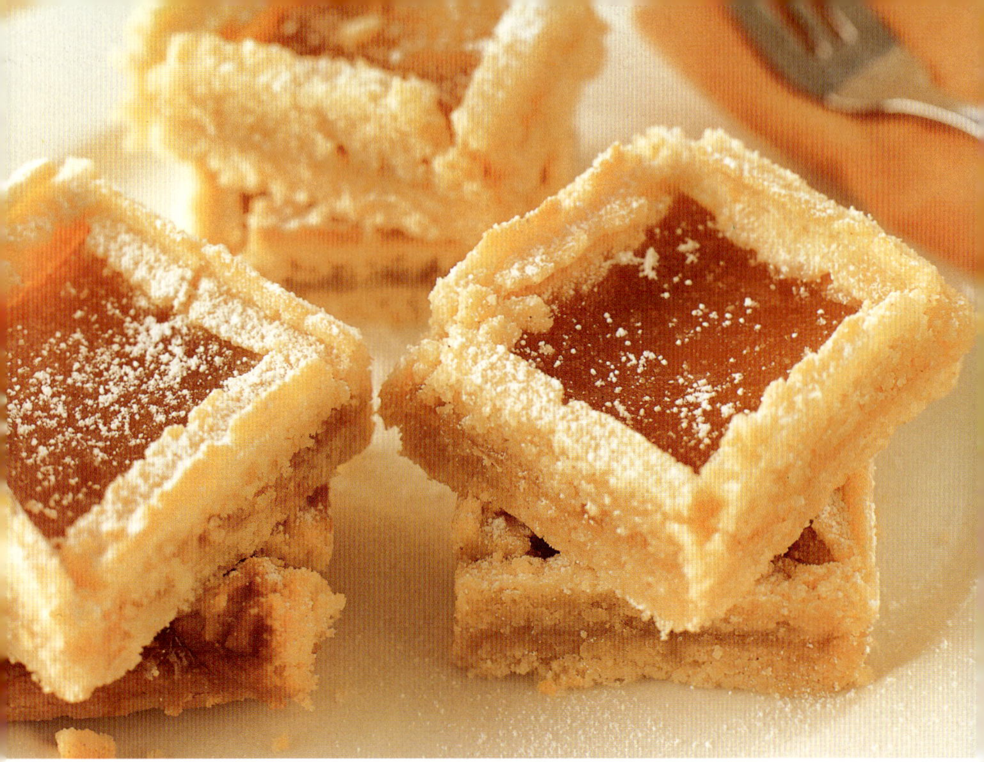
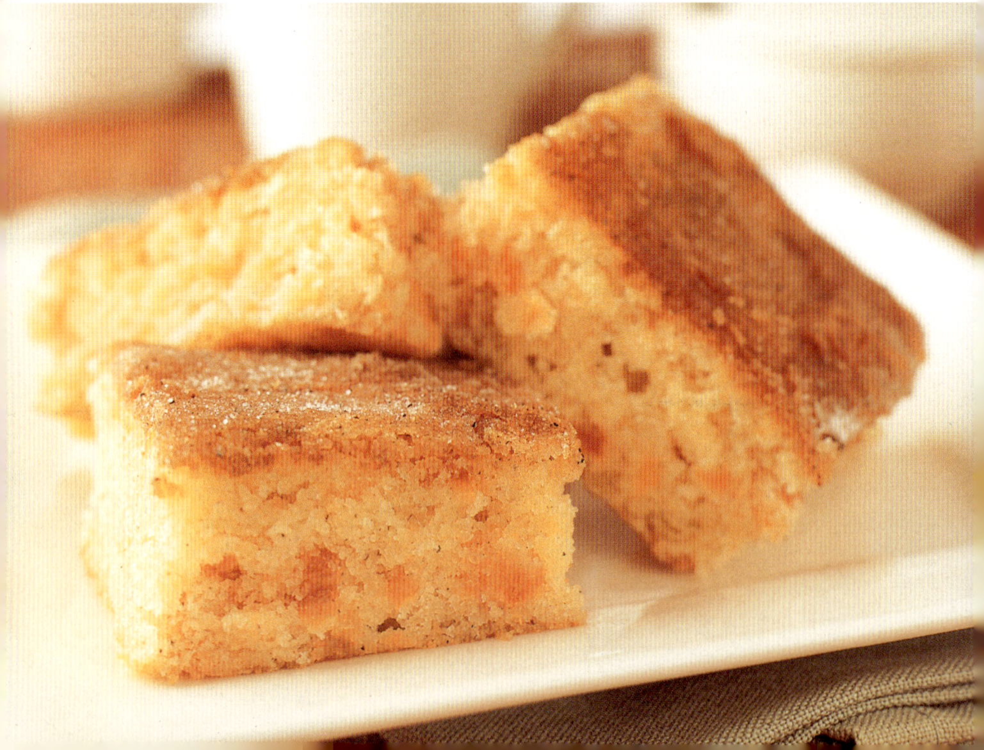

QUINCE LINZER SLICE

Prep time: 20 minutes +
  1 hour 30 minutes
  refrigeration
Cooking time: 40 minutes
Makes 16 pieces

110 g plain flour
110 g unsalted butter,
  chilled and chopped
1/4 cup (60 g) caster sugar
1 cup (110 g) ground
  almonds
1/4 teaspoon ground
  cinnamon
1 egg yolk, lightly beaten
2 teaspoons grated lemon
  rind
1 tablespoon lemon juice
200 g quince jam
icing sugar, for dusting

1 Preheat the oven to moderate 180°C (350°F/ Gas 4). Lightly grease a 20 cm square tin and line with baking paper, hanging over on two opposite sides.
2 Sift the flour into a large bowl. Rub the butter into the flour with your fingertips until it resembles fine breadcrumbs. Stir in the sugar, ground almonds and cinnamon.
3 Make a well in the centre and add the egg yolk, lemon rind and lemon juice. Mix with a flat-bladed knife, using a

Quince linzer slice (top), and Apricot and cardamom slice

cutting action, until the mixture comes together in beads. Gently gather together and place on a lightly floured work surface. Shape into a ball, flatten slightly, wrap in plastic wrap and chill for at least 1 hour.
4 Roll out two-thirds of the pastry to fit the base of the tin and place in the tin. Refrigerate for 30 minutes.
5 Prick the base all over, then spread with the jam. Pipe the remaining pastry in a lattice pattern over the top. Bake for 35–40 minutes, or until the pastry is golden brown. Dust with icing sugar while still warm.

Nutrition per piece: Fat 10 g; Protein 3 g; Carbohydrate 18 g; Dietary Fibre 1 g; Cholesterol 28.5 mg; 695 kJ (165 cal)

APRICOT AND CARDAMOM SLICE

Prep time: 15 minutes
Cooking time: 20 minutes
Makes 15 pieces

100 g finely chopped dried
  apricots
100 g unsalted butter
1 tablespoon honey
2 eggs
1/2 cup (125 g) caster sugar
3/4 cup (90 g) self-raising
  flour
1/3 cup (60 g) ground
  almonds

1 teaspoon ground
  cardamom
2 tablespoons caster sugar,
  extra
1/2 teaspoon ground
  cardamom, extra

1 Preheat the oven to moderate 180°C (350°F/ Gas 4). Lightly grease a 18 x 27 cm shallow baking tin and line the base and sides with baking paper, leaving the paper hanging over two opposites sides.
2 Place the apricots in a heatproof bowl, cover with boiling water and leave to stand for 2 minutes. Drain very well. Place the butter and honey in a saucepan over low heat until melted. Cool slightly.
3 Cream the eggs and sugar with electric beaters until light and fluffy. Fold in the butter and honey then the sifted flour, almonds, cardamom and apricots.
4 Spread evenly into the tin. Combine the extra caster sugar and cardamom and sprinkle evenly over the mixture. Bake for 20 minutes, or until cooked. Cool completely in the tin. Cut into slices.

Nutrition per piece: Fat 8.5 g; Protein 3 g; Carbohydrate 19 g; Dietary Fibre 1 g; Cholesterol 41 mg; 670 kJ (160 cal)

PEPPERMINT AND CHOCOLATE SLICE

Prep time: 20 minutes
Cooking time: 20 minutes
Makes 20 pieces

13/4 cups (220 g) plain flour
1 teaspoon baking powder
1/2 cup (95 g) soft brown sugar
180 g unsalted butter, melted
60 g white vegetable shortening (Copha)
31/2 cups (435 g) icing sugar, sifted
1 teaspoon peppermint essence
2 tablespoons milk
2 tablespoons cream
300 g dark cooking chocolate
70 g unsalted butter, extra

1 Preheat the oven to moderate 180°C (350°F/Gas 4). Grease a 20 x 30 cm baking tin and line with baking paper, hanging the paper over the two long sides.
2 Sift together the flour, baking powder and add the brown sugar. Stir in the melted butter, press into the tin and bake for 20 minutes. Cool.
3 Melt the Copha in a saucepan over medium heat. Stir in the icing sugar, peppermint, milk and cream. Mix well and pour over the pastry base. Leave to set.
4 Chop the chocolate and extra butter into small even-sized pieces and place in a heatproof bowl. Bring a saucepan of water to the boil and remove from the heat. Sit the bowl over the pan, making sure the bowl doesn't touch the water. Stand, stirring occasionally, until melted and combined. Cool slightly, then spread over the icing. Chill until set, then cut into pieces.

Nutrition per piece: Fat 18.5 g; Protein 2 g; Carbohydrate 44 g; Dietary Fibre 0.5 g; Cholesterol 34.5 mg; 1445 kJ (345 cal)

RASPBERRY AND COCONUT SLICE

Prep time: 25 minutes
Cooking time: 1 hour 25 minutes
Makes 30 pieces

21/4 cups (280 g) plain flour
3 tablespoons ground almonds
2 cups (500 g) caster sugar
250 g unsalted butter, chilled
1/2 teaspoon ground nutmeg
1/2 teaspoon baking powder
4 eggs
1 teaspoon vanilla essence
1 tablespoon lemon juice
300 g fresh or thawed frozen raspberries
1 cup (90 g) desiccated coconut
icing sugar, for dusting

1 Preheat the oven to moderate 180°C (350°F/Gas 4). Lightly grease a 20 x 30 cm shallow tin and line with baking paper, hanging over the two long sides.
2 Sift 13/4 cups (220 g) flour into a bowl. Add the almonds and 1/2 cup (125 g) caster sugar and stir to combine. Rub the butter into the flour with your fingertips until it resembles fine breadcrumbs. Press into the tin and bake for 20–25 minutes, or until golden. Reduce the oven to slow 150°C (300°F/Gas 2).
3 Sift the nutmeg, baking powder and the remaining flour onto a piece of baking paper. Beat the eggs, vanilla and remaining sugar with electric beaters for 4 minutes, or until light and fluffy. Fold in the flour with a large metal spoon. Stir in the lemon juice, raspberries and coconut and and pour over the base.
4 Bake for 1 hour, or until golden and firm. Chill in the tin, then cut into pieces. Dust with icing sugar.

Nutrition per piece: Fat 10 g; Protein 3 g; Carbohydrate 25 g; Dietary Fibre 1.5 g; Cholesterol 45 mg; 815 kJ (195 cal)

Peppermint and chocolate slice (top), and Raspberry and coconut slice

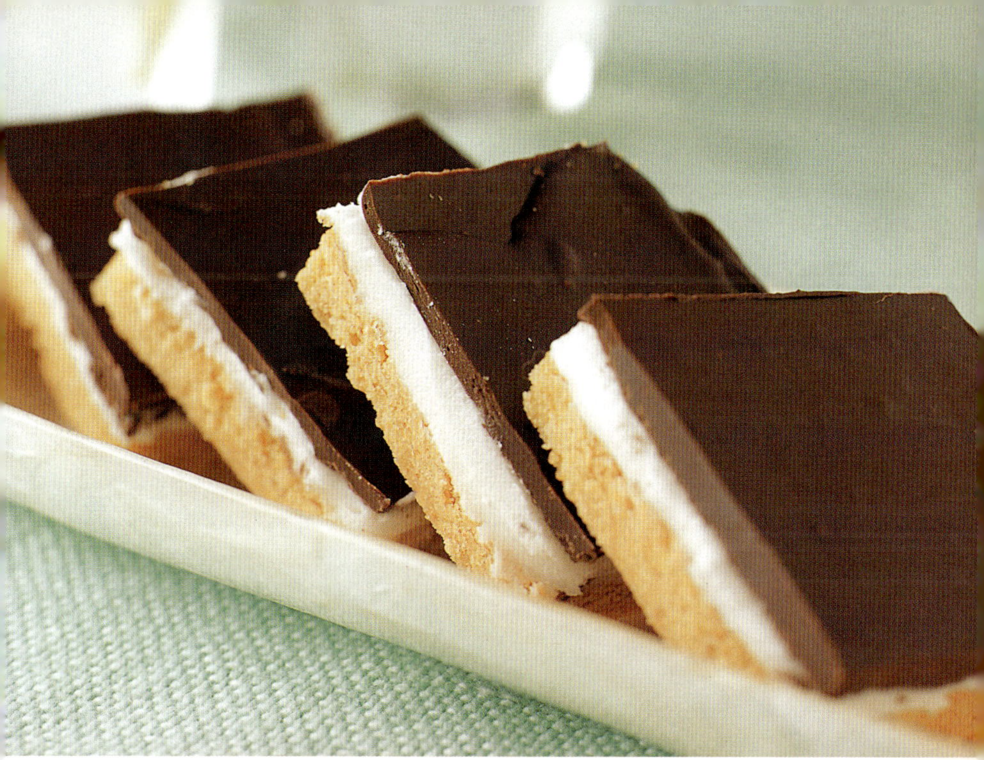

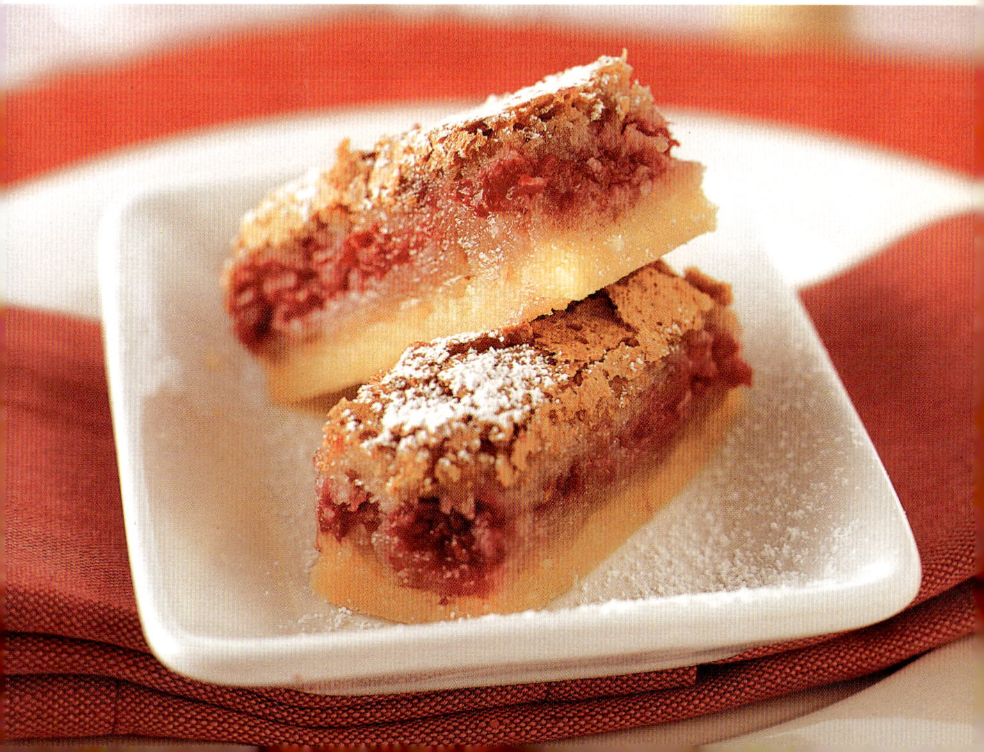

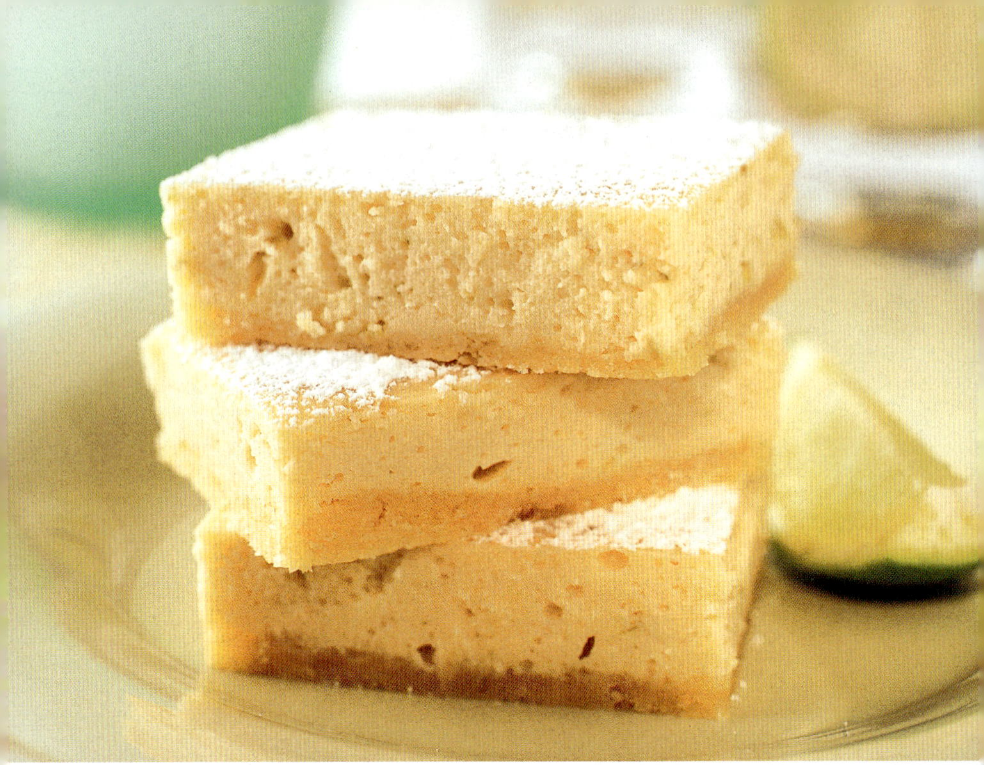

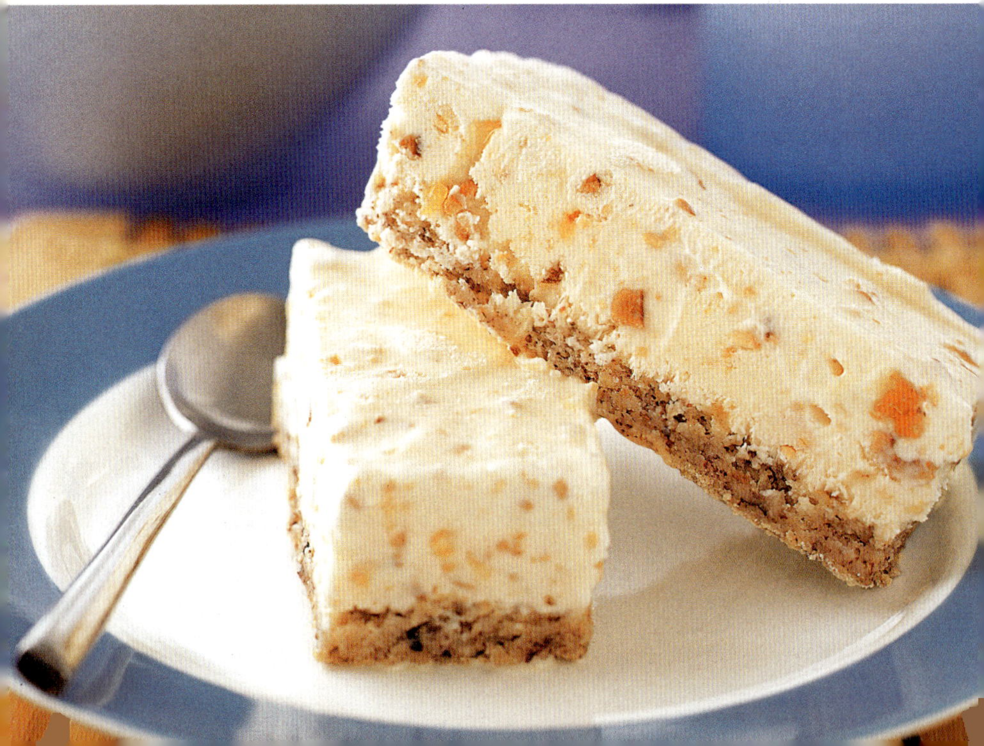

KEY LIME SLICE

Prep time: 15 minutes
Cooking time: 1 hour
Makes 12 pieces

150 g plain flour
50 g icing sugar
75 g unsalted butter, chilled
    and chopped
4 eggs
400 g can condensed milk
150 ml lime juice
1 tablespoon lime rind
icing sugar, for dusting

1 Preheat the oven to moderate 180°C (350°F/ Gas 4). Lightly grease a 18 x 27 cm baking tin and line with baking paper, hanging over the two long sides.
2 Place 100 g flour, the icing sugar and butter in a food processor and mix in short bursts until fine and crumbly. Press into the tin and bake for 12-15 minutes. Remove from the oven and leave to cool slightly. Reduce the oven to slow 150°C (300°F/Gas 2).
3 Whisk together the eggs and condensed milk, then stir in the lime juice and rind. Sift the remaining flour into the bowl, mix well and pour over the base. Bake for 30–40 minutes, or until firm. Cool

Key lime slice (top), and
Hazelnut praline
ice cream slice

completely, then cut into slices and dust with icing sugar.

Nutrition per piece: Fat 8.5 g; Protein 7 g; Carbohydrate 33 g; Dietary Fibre 0.5 g; Cholesterol 82 mg; 960 kJ (230 cal)

HAZELNUT PRALINE ICE CREAM SLICE

Prep time: 35 minutes + 4 hours freezing
Cooking time: 45 minutes
Makes 16 pieces

5 egg whites
200 g caster sugar
40 g icing sugar, sifted
30 g cornflour
110 g hazelnuts, toasted, skinned and ground
1.25 litres good-quality vanilla ice cream, softened

Praline
125 g hazelnuts, skinned
1/2 cup (125 g) sugar

1 Preheat the oven to warm 160°C (315°F/ Gas 2–3). Lightly grease a baking tray. Draw a 32 x 22 cm rectangle on baking paper, turn the paper over and use it to line the baking tray.
2 Beat the egg whites in a clean, dry bowl until soft peaks form. Add the sugar gradually and beat until thick and glossy. Lightly fold in the icing sugar, cornflour and

hazelnuts. Spread onto the baking tray, within the rectangle and smooth the surface. Bake for 30 minutes, or until lightly golden. Remove and trim the edges to fit a 20 x 30 cm baking tin. Cool completely.
3 To make the praline, spread the nuts on a lightly greased baking tray. Place the sugar and 1/4 cup (60 ml) water in a saucepan and stir over low heat until the sugar dissolves. Bring to the boil and boil without stirring until it turns a deep amber. Pour the caramel over the nuts and let it harden. Crush the praline either in a food processor using the pulse action or by wrapping the pieces in a clean tea towel and crushing with a rolling pin. Fold through the ice cream.
4 Line a 20 x 30 cm shallow tin with baking paper, hanging over on two opposite sides. Line with the meringue. Spoon the ice cream onto the meringue base, spreading evenly and smoothly. Return to the freezer for at least 4 hours before cutting into slices and serving.

Nutrition per piece: Fat 11.5 g; Protein 5 g; Carbohydrate 33 g; Dietary Fibre 1.5 g; Cholesterol 8.5 mg; 1035 kJ (245 cal)

Index

Almond chews, 4
Amaretto brownies, Chocolate and, 19
apple crumble slice, Rhubarb and, 27
Apple shortcake, 20
apple slice, Berry and, 28
Apricot and cardamom slice, 59
Apricot and macaroon slice, 44
Apricot crumble slice, 11

Bakewell slice, 31
Berry and apple slice, 28
blondies, Pecan, 36
brownies
   Chocolate and Amaretto, 19
   Classic, 7
   Mocha, 27
   Pecan, 35
   Walnut, 19

caramel shortcake, Date, 8
caramel slice, Chocolate, 28
cardamom slice, Apricot and, 59
cassata slice, Chocolate, 43
cheese slice, Passionfruit and coconut, 32
cheese swirls, Chocolate, 52
cheesecake slice, Ginger, 48
cherry slice, Cinnamon and, 36
cherry slice, Glacé, 47
Chestnut cream and chocolate slice, 55
Chewy fruit and seed slice, 39
chocolate
   and Amaretto brownies, 19
   caramel slice, 28
   cassata slice, 43
   cheese swirls, 52
   layer slice, Hazelnut meringue and, 24
   peanut squares, 48
   slice, Chestnut cream and, 55
   slice, No-bake, 23
   slice, Peppermint and, 60
   truffle macaroon slice, 16
Cider crumble slice, 44
Cinnamon and cherry slice, 36

cinnamon slice, Fig and, 8
Classic brownies, 7
coconut cheese slice, Passionfruit and, 32
coconut slice, Raspberry and, 60
crumble slice, Apricot, 11
crumble slice, Cider, 44
crumble slice, Rhubarb and apple, 27
Currant slice, 51

Date caramel shortcake, 8

Fig and cinnamon slice, 8
Florentine slice, 56
fruit and seed slice, Chewy, 39
fruit slice, Glacé, 40

Ginger cheesecake slice, 48
Ginger panforte slice, 15
ginger slice, Sesame and, 31
Glacé cherry slice, 47
Glacé fruit slice, 40

Hazelnut meringue and chocolate layer slice, 24
Hazelnut praline ice cream slice, 63

ice cream slice, Hazelnut praline, 63

Key lime slice, 63

lemon delicious slice, Passionfruit and, 40
Lemon ricotta slice, 11
Lemon squares, 47
lime slice, Key, 63
linzer slice, Quince, 59

Macadamia fingers, 7
macaroon slice, Apricot and, 44
macaroon slice, Chocolate truffle, 16
mascarpone slice, Strawberry and, 16
meringue and chocolate layer slice, Hazelnut, 24
Mocha brownies, 27

No-bake chocolate slice, 23

Orange, pistachio and semolina slice, 35

panforte slice, Ginger, 15
Passionfruit and coconut cheese slice, 32
Passionfruit and lemon delicious slice, 40
peanut squares, Chocolate, 48
Peanut toffee shortbread, 56
Pear and walnut slice, 20
Pecan blondies, 36
Pecan brownies, 35
Peppermint and chocolate slice, 60
pistachio and semolina slice, Orange, 35
Poppy seed slice, 15
praline ice cream slice, Hazelnut 63

Quince linzer slice, 59

raisin slice, Rum and, 52
Raspberry and coconut slice, 60
Rhubarb and apple crumble slice, 27
ricotta slice, Lemon, 11
Rum and raisin slice, 52

seed slice, Chewy fruit and, 39
semolina slice, Orange, pistachio and, 35
Sesame and ginger slice, 31
shortbread, Peanut toffee, 56
shortcake, Apple, 20
shortcake, Date caramel, 8
Snickerdoodle slice, 23
Sticky toffee slice, 39
Strawberry and mascarpone slice, 16

toffee shortbread, Peanut, 56
toffee slice, Sticky, 39
truffle macaroon slice, Chocolate, 16

Vanilla slice, 12

Walnut brownies, 19
walnut slice, Pear and, 20